James Casey

The Spouse of Christ

The church of the crucified

James Casey

The Spouse of Christ
The church of the crucified

ISBN/EAN: 9783741156182

Manufactured in Europe, USA, Canada, Australia, Japa

Cover: Foto ©Lupo / pixelio.de

Manufactured and distributed by brebook publishing software
(www.brebook.com)

.

James Casey

The Spouse of Christ

THE

SPOUSE OF CHRIST

OR THE

Church of the Crucified

THE

SPOUSE OF CHRIST

OR THE

Church of the Crucified

THE

SPOUSE OF CHRIST

OR

THE CHURCH OF THE CRUCIFIED

𝔄 𝔇𝔬𝔤𝔪𝔞𝔱𝔦𝔠 𝔞𝔫𝔡 𝔥𝔦𝔰𝔱𝔬𝔯𝔦𝔠 𝔓𝔬𝔢𝔪

IN FOUR PARTS.

BY THE

VERY REV. JAMES CANON CASEY, P.P.,

𝔄𝔲𝔱𝔥𝔬𝔯 𝔬𝔣

"VERSES ON DOCTRINAL AND DEVOTIONAL SUBJECTS;"
"INTEMPERANCE;" "OUR THIRST FOR DRINK;"
"TEMPERANCE SONGS AND LYRICS."

𝔓𝔞𝔯𝔱𝔰 𝔦. 𝔞𝔫𝔡 𝔦𝔦.

"Come, and I will shew thee the bride, the wife of the Lamb."
APOC. xxi. 9.

𝔇𝔲𝔟𝔩𝔦𝔫:

JAMES DUFFY & CO., LIMITED,
15 WELLINGTON QUAY.
1897.

Nihil Obstat.

G. H. MURPHY, *S.T.D.*

CENSOR THEOL. DEPUT.

Imprimatur:

✠ GULIELMUS,

ARCHIEP. DUBLINEN.

HIBERNIÆ PRIMAS.

Die 22 mens. Martii, an. 1897.

CHURCH OF THE CRUCIFIED.

𝔓art I.

DOGMATIC.

WHEN Sects and Churches everywhere abound,
How may the True among the false be found,
Since One alone can be the Spotless Bride
Of Jesus Christ whom sinners crucified?
I ask the question, as I deem it fit,
Of Christians who believe in Holy Writ;
Believe in Christ and humbly seek the way
That leads to life and to eternal day.
I ask not those who every creed disown,
And, Satan-like, would God Himself dethrone.
The men who shut their eyes against the light
Would value little what a Bard may write,
A Christian Bard, who, filled with holy fear,
Believes devoutly and with a heart sincere
The truths he utters and with love indites,
And begs God's blessing on the lines he writes.
He writes for humble souls who wisely seek
To know God's words;—to them he loves to speak;
For God conceals from haughty ones and proud
What He reveals to those among the crowd
Who humble are, with humble hearts sincere
Seek wisdom's light, and God, their Maker, fear.

A

On them kind Heaven has shed its brightest ray,
While proud philosophers but blindly stray,
And groping darkly ever miss their way;
Appearing to be gods in error's schools,
In Heaven's sight they 're nought but arrant fools.
Those men may say there is no God on high,
And every attribute to God deny;
But all in vain,—they need must have their way,
Poor silly sophists, insects of a day.
   Some men, alas! seem Atheists by choice,
And shut their ears to reason's truthful voice.
There 's no excuse, according to St. Paul,
For men who think and view our earthly ball,
And all the wonders of the starry sky,
And yet th' existence of a God deny!
What swain untutored views the orb of day,
The countless stars that pave the Milky Way,
The earth's rotation and the wondrous laws
That regulate the Universe, but draws   •
The right conclusion, true to reason's sight,—
There is a God of Wisdom infinite,
Who made the earth and all that move thereon,
And all the lights that on the earth have shone;
The sun, the moon, the stars serenely bright,
Those lamps divine that guide our steps by night,
All which proclaim a Great and Primal Cause,
Who made all creatures and who gave them laws,
While over all Omnipotence presides,
And Wisdom infinite unerring guides,
Directing all, since all on Him depend,
Unto some noble and exalted end.
This Cause upholds and orders all things right,
As must be manifest to reason's sight.

Can feeble man those attributes deny
To Him who made the earth and starry sky,
And planned the Universe so rich, so grand,
The wondrous work of an Almighty Hand?
If senseless atheists should dare advance
That all we see is but the work of chance,
For such I write not, but most humbly pray
Kind Heaven may shed a bright supernal ray
Upon their souls to guide their steps aright,
As Faith infused must give the needed light.
Poor reason's eye is far too weak and frail,
To see beyond or penetrate the veil.

The Church of Christ in Heaven's wondrous plan
Alone can save the race of fallen man.
That Church divine, whatever some may say,
Was never meant to lead poor souls astray.
The Church Christ built—His followers to save—
Can never be the sport of wind and wave
On error's sea, by every tempest toss'd;
Not so false churches which, alas! are lost;
For without faith they cannot reach the shore
Where all is bliss, and sorrows are no more.
None, none, can God, their loving Maker, please
Without true Faith, or cross life's stormy seas
So as to gain the wished-for port of rest,
And share the joys of all the saints and blest.

False churches are the work of man and frail,
And vainly struggle 'gainst fierce error's gale;
No chart or compass, no unfailing skill,
No power divine to bid the waves be still!
Those fragile barks, the work of human pride,
Go down before the tempest and the tide!

To them was never promised aid divine,
To bear them safely o'er the stormy brine;
To Peter's barque alone such aid is given,
And all the rest upon the rocks are driven;
And, floundering, sink beneath the rolling waves,
The fate of heresy's unhappy slaves.

  Christ built His Church upon a solid rock,
A keep and shelter for His faithful flock;
He built a Church that shall for ever stand,
Which could not be if built on moving sand.
Our Lord foresaw what powers would assail
And would o'erthrow if error could prevail;
Foresaw the strength of all the gates of hell,
And all that would against the Church rebel.
He saw the subtlety of Satan's pride,
And all the wicked that would take his side;
He saw the heresies that would arise,
And would His Vicar, and Himself despise,
And built His Church their efforts to withstand,
And show the work of His Almighty Hand;
And prove to every age her Builder's skill,
And His Omnipotence to work His will.

  Let all who would the Church of Jesus find
Approach and search with simple, upright mind,
And ask of God the light divine that leads
The soul aright amidst conflicting creeds;
And from the truths of Revelation see
What ought the Church of Christ for ever be;
What are its MARKS, as in the Scripture shown,
Those Marks, by which Christ's Church is ever known.
For fallen man, so erring and so blind,
The Church must not be difficult to find;

Else some are not accountable who stray,
And some who never find the narrow way.
The Church must then to earnest men appear
For ever visible, for ever clear,
And making evident as stars that shine,
No hand hath made her but a hand divine.

If wanting faith, no mortal can be saved,
And if by heresy hell's streets are paved,
And if the Faith no church can teach but *one*,
It should be visible as is the sun,
That earnest souls may never miss the road,
That leads by faith to Heaven's blest abode.
If some there are who seek and fail to find,
They're men whom pride and sins of malice blind;
If they find not they have themselves to blame,
They love the darkness, and must bear the shame.

The Church of Christ must *everlasting be*
As well as *visible* for all to see,
For Christ has promised She shall never fail,
And that her enemies shall not prevail;
That He Himself shall with His Church remain,
To guide, enlighten, nourish and sustain:
And that the Holy Spirit shall preside
O'er all her teaching, and divinely guide.
His Church He placed beyond dark error's reach
And made *infallible;* she cannot teach
But truth divine which she received to hold,
And to dispense to all the Christian fold.
The everlasting Church must last for aye,
And ever keep her enemies at bay;
Must guard the faith of Christ with loving care,
And guard His followers from every snare

Of schism, heresy, and error vain
Which would her faith destroy or morals stain.
  The Word of God makes patent as the sun
The Church of God, Christ's Holy Spouse, is *One*.
One Church is spoken of, and one alone,
As built by Christ; no other shall He own,
(On Peter built, Himself the corner stone).
One Faith, one Lord, one kingdom, and one fold,
One Church divine the faithful flock to hold,
One Tree that shelters all the birds of air,
One Pillar strong truth's lights divine to bear.
The Church is likened to a fountain sealed,
Now to a vineyard, now a single field,
And every figure to the Church applied,
Shows Christ has only *One* celestial bride.
Noah built no second Ark to save
Both man and beast from the engulphing wave;
Though other boats were drawn along the beach,
From Peter's only Christ vouchsafed to teach.
The Church of Christ, however widely spread,
Has but one body, having but one Head,
Which, like the human, with its members all,
Forms but one whole, according to St. Paul.
If through the inspired page our eyes we run,
The Church of Christ is always ever *One;*
And if inquirers ever feel a doubt,
They 're bound to search and find that true one out;
And view with simple and unjaundiced eye,
And Scripture texts with earnest minds apply;
And if they do, they cannot fail to see
How wondrous is the Church's unity.
One Founder has the Church, one final end,
One Head on earth to guard her and defend,

To whom her children fond allegiance own—
(To him who sits on Peter's royal throne)
To whom our Lord entrusted all His flock,
And gave the Keys His Kingdom to unlock.
Her public worship, and her every rite,
Show forth Christ's Church as visible and bright—
The source and centre of religious light.
    The Church in Faith and discipline is One,
In what to follow and in what to shun;
Her Holy Bible and Tradition sound
For ever showing where salvation's found.
    Christ's Church with *Holiness* must ever shine,
And show by this her origin divine.
The prophet called the Church a holy way,
And such it was, and such it is to-day,
And such it will be till the world shall end,
And all the just shall with our Lord ascend;
Holiness becomes the House of Him
Who is adored by Saint and Cherubim.
St. Paul has said, and no one can deny,
Christ loved His Church, and died to sanctify
His spotless Spouse, which shall for aye remain
His loving Bride, not knowing spot or stain.
"Time writes no wrinkle on her agèd brow;"
Such as St. Paul beheld her she is now.
Her Lord has left her *Means* to sanctify
Her children all, and fit them for the sky.
But yet we oft unholy children meet,
For tares will ever grow among the wheat,
And many scandals, till the day of doom,
Shall in her vineyard like wild nettles bloom.
E'en in the miracles the Saviour wrought,
Bad fishes were as well as good ones caught.

In God's own house are vessels made of gold,
And vessels also of inferior mould;
But those of gold shall never, never fail
T' enrich God's house and for its use avail.
In every age bright Saints in her shall live,
And praise and glory to her Founder give.
If some are bad, and still to badness prone
Despite the Church, the fault is all their own.
They hear her words, and hearing disobey,
Indulge their passions and neglect to pray,
To curb the tongue and turn away the eye,
And fail the sinful flesh to mortify.
   From time to time, as Christ Himself foretold,
Great miracles are wrought within the fold
By saintly souls, whom holy zeal inspires
To call on God when God's own truth requires
To be confirmed by wonders from on high,
To prove its truth and make the demons fly.
Great miracles beyond a shade of doubt
Which raise the dead and drive the demons out,
Convince the pagan, lead him to embrace
The Truth of God dispensing light and grace.
   The Church is holy in her Head divine,
And must with holiness for ever shine,
And holy in her doctrine, and must teach
True holiness to all within her reach.
All souls that shall her holy doctrine hear
With docile hearts, and with a will sincere,
Shall do God's will, and keep His holy laws,
And in well-doing never stop or pause;
Shall mourn their sins with humble hearts contrite,
And make God's word their study and delight;

Shall fast and pray, and daily mortify
The sinful flesh, and every danger fly,
And shall excel in faith, and hope, and love,
And place their treasures in their home above—
All such are Saints, and ever shall be found,
Within the Church where holy souls abound.

The Church of Christ I from the Scriptures see,
Must have the note of *Catholicity.*
When Christ had come the race of man to save,
He to th' Apostles this commission gave :—
"Go teach *all nations all* you've heard from Me,
And with you teaching I shall ever be."
(The Apostles were, like other men, to die,
But other bishops shall their place supply
To teach and preach, still aided from on high.)
And they went forth the gospel light to spread,
And Christ rich blessings on their labours shed,
While they wrought miracles and raised the dead.
They preached to all, and every danger braved,
Converting daily such as should be saved.
The Church increased and grew from side to side,
And spread its fruitful branches far and wide.
'Tis clear to all from history's truthful page,
How well the Church has spread from age to age.
The words of God to Abraham old addressed,
"In thee shall all the kindred of the earth be blessed,"
Have been and must be ever verified,
And hence the Church must spread both far and wide,
And through successive ages to the end,
Till Christ to judge shall from His Throne descend.

The stone that Daniel saw—a mountain made,
Cut from the mountain without human aid,

And growing large until the earth it filled,
Points out to all, no matter how unskill'd,
That Christ's own Church prefigured by that stone
Must grow and spread itself from zone to zone,
And hence the Church of God must spread through time,
In every country and in every clime.
The Church that does not wide its branches spread
Is not Christ's Church, but one whose roots are dead.
And so Christ's Church, in every age and clime,
Has preached and preaches all His words sublime,
Concealing nothing that her Saviour taught,
And working wonders as her Master wrought.
To what the Lord had taught His Spouse to say,
She nothing adds and nothing takes away.
If doubts arise she will the truth define,
And tell her children what is truth divine,
And what is error that they may not stray
From Heaven's path and miss the narrow way,
'Tis hers to guard the treasures which He gave, .
And to dispense them to His Flock, and save
From error, darkness, and the snares of hell,
That they hereafter may with angels dwell.
Christ gave His Church the vigour to expand
And spread its branches wide through every land.
The Church that does so, is, we all believe,
The Church of Christ which never can deceive.
His Church shall last until the stars shall fall,
And death and judgment see the end of all.
No length of years shall quench the blessèd light
Which Christ first lighted, and which burns more bright
As ages roll and empires pass away,
And all things else betoken swift decay.

That fire divine shall never cease to burn
Till Christ our Judge shall to the earth return,
To judge the world and all His servants crown,
And send the wicked to hell's prison down.
The Church of Christ in every age and place,
Must her existence to the Saviour trace
And His Apostles, and must prove her claim
To *Apostolical*—the very same
That Christ had built upon a rock of old,
While head succeeds to head and fold to fold,
The first to rule, the latter to obey,
"While generations in their course decay,"
And pointing out in one unbroken line
Of Heads Supreme her origin divine.
Her doctrine, discipline, and worship grand
Alone defying time's unsparing hand,
And ever holding universal sway,
While thrones and kingdoms totter to decay;
And all false churches that have sprung from pride,
Are swept away and buried in the tide;
But she shall stand till Christ comes down in might,
To call the just and place them on His right,
And place the bad—ah! sad it is to tell—
Upon His left whence they are dragged to hell!
The Church must on her old foundation stand
As shaped and fashioned by her Maker's hand;
Her doctrine, mission, Orders—all must tell
That Christ, her Architect, had built her well;
And that her faith, no "reformation" needs,
As age to age and priest to priest succeeds.
Her Orders give her a succession true
Of Ministers to enlighten and renew

The war with error she must ever wage
In every country and in every age.
Succeeding Ministers must still remain
As links of one, unbroken, wondrous chain;
No link e'er missing to enchain the flock
To blessed Peter, who was made the Rock,
For whom Christ prayed his faith should never fail,
E'en though hell's powers should its strength assail.
No length of years shall quench the blessèd light
Which Christ first lighted but to burn more bright;
That flame divine shall never cease to burn
Till Christ our Judge shall to our earth return.
The Church of Christ in near and distant lands
Must ever show the rock on which she stands;
That rock which ever wind and wave defies,
No matter how the stormy billows rise
To surge around it and to roar in vain,
Unmoved and solid shall it still remain
The Church of God to strengthen and sustain.
The Church which Scripture likens to a tree
Must show connection with the Holy See,
That all who see its Apostolic fruit,
Must know its seed, its Planter, and its root;
And must confess, as they its grandeur see,
There's not on earth but one such holy tree.
    When Christ had sent His chosen Twelve to go
And preach His word, the heavenly seed to sow,
He gave them proofs of love and loving care,
And bade them all of wicked men beware;
That in return for zealous labours great,
They would receive a wicked world's dread hate—
A world which ever persecutes the just,
And which His followers should never trust.

He cautioned prudence, told them not to fear,
But preach His word, and preaching persevere;
And He 'd reward them in His home above
For all their labours and for all their love.

    And then again does not th' Apostle Paul
Declare th' Apostles last and least of all,
And made a spectacle to all the world,
As they before its wicked eyes unfurled
Christ's royal banner and upreared the Cross,
While they were treated as the merest dross,
Reviled, dishonoured, persecuted, scorned,
While crowns and laurels wicked brows adorned?
And so the world—a world of pride and lust—
Has ever treated righteous souls and just;
Hence *Persecution* ever seems to me
The Church's mark as well as Sanctity,
Or any other of those marks divine
Which show the Church and point to Peter's line;
And I for one shall this last note apply,
As I on Churches cast a glancing eye.

    If we one Church, and one alone, can find,
That has the marks by Christ Himself designed,
To point her out as His to all who seek—
To docile souls and humble hearts and meek;
Aye seek the truth with pure and simple mind—
Since pride and lust are ever sure to blind—
That Church is Christ's we hold and must believe,
For God does not and never can deceive;
And if we find the world to rail and hate,
And make her suffer persecutions great;
And if that Church maintains an endless fight
With error dark, still spreading Gospel light,

Converting barbarous nations far and near,
Baptizing, preaching, filling men with fear
Of God and judgment, if they live in sin,
Exhorting all the joys of heaven to win,
And raising fallen nature from the mire
Of sin and ignorance, and casting fire
Upon the earth—the fire of love divine—
Which burns the dross and doth the gold refine,
The lamp of science feeding well with oil,
And raising up the hapless sons of toil;
Exalting woman to her proper sphere,
And loving justice with a love sincere,
And overcoming all the gates of hell,
Whose strength and malice it were long to tell,
While round her battlements her foes engage
With hate undying and relentless rage,
But failing still her faith to undermine,—
Men must confess that Church to be divine,
And all must own she is the Spotless Bride
Of Jesus Christ whom Pilate crucified.

What Church but *Rome's*, and search the nations round,
Can show the *Marks* that ever must be found
In Christ's own Church, in every age that rolls,
And every land between the distant Poles.
She is in Faith united to the Rock,
On which Christ built His Church;—her flock
Believe the same, and nought as dogma hold
That is not held by all her faithful fold;
Their faith the same as in the days of old.

The Church of Rome throughout all nations spread
Is always *One* united to one Head—
A Head that rules supreme from sea to sea,
Preserving order, strength, and unity.

His words are never in the least gainsaid,
His precepts all most lovingly obeyed,
His person loved, though by th' ungodly feared,
His blessing sought for and himself revered.
No words can tell the fond affection shown
To him who sits upon the Papal throne
By million souls, who willingly obey
The Pope of Rome and filial homage pay:—
Aye, million souls from every nation sprung
Throughout the world and speaking every tongue.
What other church can point to such as he?
What other flock can show such unity?
They're one in faith, they all believe the same
Old truths divine that from th' Apostles came;
The same their Sacraments, in number seven,
Which cleanse, make strong, and fit the soul for heaven,
And from the rising to the setting sun
They have *One* Sacrifice and only *One*,
So that the faithful through what lands they pass
May all unite and offer up the Mass;
And may, though cast upon a foreign shore,
Their hidden God at Holy Mass adore,
And all receive Him—greatest gift divine—
Beneath the humble veils of bread and wine.

One faith have all the children of the Pope.
They're one in faith, and one in holy hope;
The same belief whate'er the foe may think,
As all do from the same pure fountain drink.
If any shall the heavenly draught refuse,
He is cut off and 'tis a gain to lose.
An unbeliever who is wanting found,
Is a withered limb both rotten and unsound.

The Church of Rome, and time has proved her wise, ⎫
Shall never yield to force or compromise   ⎬
One particle of Truth, or favour lies.   ⎭
Not so with heresies, which quickly pass,
And melt like snow, or wither like the grass;
They pass away, and like the hollow wind,
Leave nothing but a blasted name behind,
And errors which perchance awhile may last,
And o'er the globe their blighting shadows cast.
    The Catholic Church is *Holy*—holy, quite,
The source and centre of religious light
To all the world—'twas so in ages past,
And shall in future—long as time shall last.
If by its fruit we're told to judge the tree,
The Church of Rome, as every one may see,
Has holy been—aye ever since her birth,
And is the only holy Church on earth;
The only Church that had a holy Head,
The only one with holy doctrine fed,
The only one whose doctrine knows no taint,
The only one that ever made a Saint,
The only one that teaches to abstain,
To fast, to mortify and to restrain
The carnal appetites, and curbing, tame
Rebellious passions, and can quench their flame,
Unruly passions, turbulent and strong,
That drag the sinner in directions wrong;
The only Church that really combats vice,
And daily offers holy sacrifice,
And gives her children th' angelic bread,
By which their souls are fortified and fed;
The only Church that ever stemmed the waves
Of persecution, and that freed the slaves;

That taught the nations, and that spread the light
Of science when the world was dark as night;
That raised great monasteries the light to spread,
Where scholars studied and the poor were fed,
And strangers harboured without charge or fee,
And all found shelter, kindness, charity.

Her holy children strongest proofs supply
How well she can her members sanctify
Who hear her words with docile hearts and pure,
And quit their sins salvation to secure.

Where can, I ask, and search the world around,
One thousand holy, learned, men be found
That can with Rome's great prelates be compared,
Who have such gifts of grace and nature shared?
Outside the Church what prelates can be named
For science, holiness, and learning famed,
Like those of Rome, through every country spread,
And all united with the Pope as Head?
Though differing wide, in language, country, race,
They're one in faith which one and all embrace,
And all obedient to their Head Supreme
And caring little for the world's esteem—
A world in wickedness and folly sunk,
With pride, and lust, and avarice, made drunk!
Those thousand * prelates lead a holy life,
And have no care for riches, child, or wife,
As have the prelates of another creed—
Good fathers, husbands, loving ones indeed,

---

* The *Irish Catholic Directory* sets down the number of Residential Sees as 966. This does not include districts governed by Prefects Apostolic and Apostolic Vicars who exercise episcopal functions and jurisdiction under the *Propaganda*.

B

41

And most of whom lead decent moral lives,
And quite enamoured of their pious wives,
And quite uxorious I freely own,
While Popish Prelates care for God alone,
And for His holy worship and the poor,
Their sole inheritance, their only cure.
For them no balls, no banquets, no carouse,
T' advance their daughters, or to please their spouse,
To get their sons upon the golden shelves
Of rich preferment, as they find themselves.
The Popish Prelates seek a higher meed,
And leave to bishops of another creed
The world's enjoyments which they love and prize,
And which are charming in a layman's eyes;
For these the Shepherds of an erring fold
Are nought but laymen if the truth were told.
It has been proved, and Catholics believe,
No valid orders * did they e'er receive.
No fast for them, for feasting is their call,
No single life, though lauded by St. Paul,
As farthest from domestic care and strife,
And suiting best an Apostolic life,
For that would savour (fortunate excuse)
Of Popish error and of " foul abuse."
If this be sanctity 'twill cause surprise,
Dispel old prejudices, and ope the eyes
Of silly Papists who do marriage shun,
With greater freedom after Christ to run,
To love God more and love the creature less,
To serve the poor, and mitigate distress,

---

* Since these lines were written Rome has spoken and pronounced
Anglican Orders invalid.

To cast more wide the fire of holy love,
And fit poor souls for heaven's courts above.
  Behold Rome's clergymen in every grade,
Or in the world, or in the cloister's shade,
Who vowed to fly the world and marriage shun,
And lead the lives of holy Monk and Nun,
To serve the Lord and greater graces share,
Relieved from anxious and domestic care,
And often trouble and domestic strife,
From disagreement between man and wife.
Are they not better in their Maker's sight,
And better fitted to maintain the fight
With sin and Satan, that most potent foe,
That seeks man's ruin, and the overthrow
Of virtue, piety, and all that's chaste,
And strives to make our earth a moral waste?
See how Rome's clergy spend their valued time
In prayer and praise, in checking sin and crime,
And giving, by their holy lives and state,
To all their people an example great
Of self-denial, piety, and praise,
Of prayerful nights and of laborious days,
Of study, penance, and incessant toil,
And all to fill their burning lamps with oil;
And teaching souls all sin and guilt to fly
To do God's work, and seek his bliss on high.
  Can married clergy do their work so well?
Let those who know and let experience tell.
Can he on Sunday from distraction keep
Whose wife is dead, whose children wail and weep?
Can he with eloquence in preaching glow
Whose children are in typhus fever low?

Can he with willing, fervent step, and quick,
Pay zealous visits to the poor and sick?
Can he with fervour soothe the dying bed
Of one in fever 'mid contagion dread,
While he is thinking of his little flock,
And fears contagion clinging to his frock?
Can he his Church adorn and beautify
Who scarcely can his children's needs supply?

The priest who vows to God a single life
Has nought to dread concerning child or wife,
But does his duty fearing not to die,
Should heaven call him to his home on high
Before his time; if God should so decree,
He has no thought but to his God to flee.

But some may say and reason too allows,
Not every Priest or Friar keeps his vows;
And if they don't why praise the single state,
Or censure those who seek a godly mate?
Some priests there are who never get a call
To such a state, and consequently fall;
But all must own the number is but small.
And some who get a call and do embrace,
May fall through sin and the abuse of grace,
And give great scandal as we sometimes see,
(And Christ foretold that scandals great must be;
That tares shall ever grow among the wheat,
And hence the Church has scandals great to meet);
But such ne'er rob her of her sanctity;
She has no share in their iniquity.
Poor Judas got a call in days of old,
And yet his Lord and loving Master sold;
But should his sin affect the good eleven,
Who faithful stood and now are crowned in Heaven;

While hapless Judas did his birthright sell,
And by his sin has purchased death and hell?
And so may others, till earth's final day,
Abuse God's grace, and from it fall away.
But then should he who runs the race and wins,
Be made to answer for another's sins?
Who had no share in others' sins at all,
Nor gave occasion for another's fall,
Must not for others blame or censure bear,
Since in their sins he had nor part nor share.
When all that he could do was to lament
The sins and scandals he could not prevent.
    And whose again have been the holy throngs
Of holy souls who sing their matin songs
In cloistered homes, in those monastic cells,
" Where heavenly, pensive contemplation dwells !"
To which chaste virgins all their treasures bring,
To lay before their Saviour and their King,
And who leave ease and luxury behind,
A pillow hard and humble fare to find?
An humble cell of every comfort bare,
Is all the luxury they have to share !
Some spend their hours in contemplation sweet,
In spirit prostrate at their Saviour's feet,
While meditating on His love for man,
And on the mercies of Redemption's plan,
And the atonement He for sinners made,
When by His Blood He all our ransom paid,
And gave His Church a legacy divine,
Beneath the lowly veils of Bread and Wine,
To be our food, our strength, our light, and guide,
When our frail barques encounter wind and tide

On life's rough sea, when pirates strong assail,
Amid the terrors of the wrecking gale :
Without that help we could not reach the coast
When thus pursued by hell's infernal host,
But strengthened by the holy, heavenly bread
We sail secure, and no disaster dread.
On subjects such as these they love to dwell
Which light with love divine their silent cell.
These, like to Mary, choose the better part,
The love of God possessing all their heart.
    Others, like Martha, active toil combine
With meditation on God's truths divine.
These teach the ignorant, the vicious mend,
The needful succour, and the sick attend,
Assist the dying, and console the sad,
The good encourage, and reform the bad ;
And e'en 'mid pestilence and carnage fly
To teach the sick and wounded how to die !
For them no terrors hath contagion dread,
They view the image of their Saviour dead,
And all their fears before that image fly,
They're all for God, and care not when they die.
Now think of all the holy labour done
By good religious, whether Monk or Nun ;
See how they teach the children of the poor,
And make their lot more happy and secure.
See how good Brothers teach the humble boy,
From motives pure, which never know alloy,
Whose holy charity and burning zeal
Bring countless blessings on the common weal,
By teaching humble boys exposed to vice
Religion, science, morals, good and nice,

And helping them an eminence to gain
Which of themselves they never could attain,
And keeping them from evil paths that lure
To sin and crime the children of the poor!
You'd know those children as they walk the street,
Respectful, modest, tidy and discreet;
Their very manners indicate a mind
Above their station—chastened and refined.
Men cannot see—'tis God alone that knows—
The good such teaching on the poor bestows.

And zealous ladies even monks surpass,
In teaching females of the humbler class,
As well as ladies of the upper ranks
Who best can show their gratitude and thanks;
But joys eternal shall reward the care
Of training children desolate and bare.

What other Church can show such teaching zeal,
What other teachers such devotion feel,
For works of charity so nobly done
By good religious—whether Monk or Nun?

The Catholic Church which came from God on High
Is given alone the *means* to sanctify
The head, the heart, the intellect, the will,
Of all her sons, whatever state they fill.
'Tis she preserved the Word of God from taint,
That Word that gave her many a blessed Saint.

She has the holy Sacraments t' efface
The stains of sin, and pour out floods of grace.
Has Baptism true to cleanse from Adam's sin,
Which gives a title man could never win
To joys eternal which we could not see,
Had Christ not died poor fallen man to free

From sin and death and from the chains of hell,
And make him worthy with Himself to dwell,
In bliss and glory 'bove the sun and sky,
And joys eternal which shall never die.

And Penance next restoring to us all
The merits lost when into sin we fall,
Which helps the soul lost graces to regain,
And strength to fight till triumph we obtain.

And here I pause, and here I fain would tell,
What countless souls Confession keeps from hell,
And helps to keep upon the narrow road
That leads to Heaven's blissful blest abode.
What is it keeps the young and guileless mind
So chaste, so pure, so holy, so refined
In thought, and sentiment, and at an age
When strong temptations and the demons wage
Their fiercest war against the young unstained
And unsuspecting—yet unchained
By sinful habits and by Satan's chains,
Which hell has forged to multiply its gains ?
What is it which when souls have left the track
Of godliness, recalls and brings them back
And rescues them from Satan's cunning snare,
And teaches them of dangers to beware,
And tells of Satan's dark deceitful guile
And of his agent's tempting, luring smile,
And lying promises that tempt—decoy
The souls of youth to murder and destroy ?
Confession saves them from a thousand ills,
And pious maxims into youth instils,
Plucks out the weeds of evil as they show
Above the ground to spring apace and grow.

'Tis in Confession Heaven doth provide
For simple souls a father and a guide,
With knowledge dowered and inflamed with zeal,
And one who does for all his children feel,
Who knows the malice of their dreadful foes,
And points the path to penitents, and shows
How they may tame the passions that rebel,
And fly occasions that lead on to hell:
How they may keep from Satan's wily snares,
May weed their souls of hurtful, sinful tares;
How they should sin and its allurement shun,
And for the prize as Christian Athletes run;
And how they should both meditate and pray,
Subdue the flesh and drive the foe away.
This guide is also a physician mild
To heal the wounds of every erring child,
Who has for troubled souls a healing balm,
And knows temptations' stormy winds to calm.
How happy they to whom kind Heaven sends
A holy guide, the best of faithful friends.
　　Confession, which has been so long assailed
By Protestants, who miserably failed
This means of sanctity to undermine—
A means most holy, fruitful, and divine,
A means productive of the greatest good,
A means repugnant unto flesh and blood,
And hence for ages it could never stand
Had it not come from God's Almighty Hand—
Is finding favour now on English ground,
Which lately hated it with hate profound;
And English parsons now restore its use,
Who lately loaded it with foul abuse;

And now confess their fathers acted wrong
To part with what was powerful and strong
To hinder vices, and which helped to sow
The seeds of virtue, and to make them grow,
While its removal filled the land with ills,
With vice that poisons and with sin that kills
Domestic virtue both in young and old,
Till Christian morals fly the Christian fold,
And sins unnumbered fill and overflow
A land so holy centuries ago!
And thus it is that error runs its course,
And truth returns with redoubled force
Till those embrace it who had shunned before,
And their past errors and past sins deplore.
    The greatest means of sanctity and best
Is Christ Himself, who left a great bequest
Unto His Church the night before He died,
A wondrous gift, and one that sanctified
His faithful followers in every age :—
The swain untutored and the learnèd sage,
The holy hermit and the son of toil,
Who works his day and fructifies the soil ;
The saintly Bishop and the holy Nun,
Who to the odour of Christ's garments run,
The humble peasant and the simple clown,
The royal head that wears a golden crown,
Are all made holy by this gift divine,
Which doth to goodness all their hearts incline.
All are invited to this Banquet spread
In Christ's own Church where holy souls are fed
With Christ's own Body 'neath the form of bread,
And with His Blood beneath the form of wine,
And all made strong with nourishment divine,

Which cleanses, comforts, strengthens, sanctifies
Poor weary souls, and fits them for the skies.
  The English Protestants not long ago
Blasphemed the Eucharist, as all men know.
I well remember in my early years
The horrid blasphemies that pierced my ears,
And never dreamed I'd see it come to pass
That English Parsons would restore the Mass,
That is, as far as ceremonies go,
And words, and actions, but the faithful know
They lack the power to consecrate—alas!
And do at best but imitate the Mass,
Until, perhaps, they get the greater grace,
And they the faith of Holy Church embrace.
  This shows how truth will in the end prevail,
How long so e'er its enemies assail,
And persecute the Church for conscience' sake
With fire, and sword, with faggot and with stake.
The Church still lives and shall men's needs supply,
But pampered heresy is doomed to die.
The child of pride, of avarice and lust,
May live awhile, but die in time it must.
  Another *Means* of Holiness and great
Is holy marriage for the married state,
A state in which the largest numbers live,
And praise and glory to their Maker give,
While some—the few—to high perfection tend,
And ne'er beneath the yoke of marriage bend,
To serve their God with greater liberty,
From marriage cares and all distraction free ;
But all depends upon the special call
Men get from God, the loving Lord of all ;

That call should not be slighted or ignored,
That God may be in every state adored.
The marriage state is holy, giving grace
To those so called, and who that state embrace.
What Church but Rome's has honoured married life,
And so prepares the husband and the wife ·
To enter piously with chaste intent,
And to receive this Holy Sacrament,
Which gives the married graces great to bear
The yoke of marriage, and devoutly rear
Their holy offspring heaven's bliss to share.

To civil courts they never have recourse
T' obtain through guilt a legalized divorce,
Like English Protestants so rich and wise,
Who in their pride the Popish creed despise,
Who never blush, it seems, nor dread disgrace
To publish infamies to make a case!
T' obtain divorce and break the marriage tie,
Which none can break until one partner die,
Unless the Church and Holy Scriptures lie.
When marriage is by wicked laws defiled,
Who then to virtue can train up the child?
And how can parents separated wide
Their shame and guilt from their young offspring hide?
Can those who thus a sad example show
Point to the child the way it ought to go?

If public virtues from domestic spring,
And if on kingdoms virtues blessings bring,
And if divorces poison virtue's source,
Can sanctity be born of divorce?   ·
And will not chastity and virtue die,
Where none respect the sacred marriage tie?

'Tis vain to look for sanctity or saint,
Where such abuses public morals taint.
  Now, if of Heaven, prayer be the key,
A potent *means* of grace and sanctity,
Look round among your churches all and say,
What men but Catholics devoutly pray ?
And who, like them, this holy means employs,
Which strengthens faith and unbelief destroys ?
Some think much confidence enough to save,
And there 's no need of God or Saint to crave,
Of God to bless, of Saints to intercede,
And for their clients and their kindred plead.
Belief, they think, without good works, will save,
And bring to glory as they cross the grave !
'Tis only Papists, with exceptions rare,
That have recourse to strong incessant prayer,
To worship God, to thank Him and adore,
To seek His grace, and mercy to implore,
To sing His praises, and to beg His aid
Against man's foe in panoply arrayed
To ruin Adam's weak and erring race,
So sure to yield without the help of grace.
  While other Churches give but Sabbath days
To prayer, worship, adoration, praise,
(And without faith, how little these avail,
We know from Paul, and Paul is never stale).
The Church of Rome, as fits the gate of Heaven,
Opes wide her Churches every day in seven,
And offers unto God the " Clean Oblation,"
Inviting to it every rank and station.
Both rich and poor from every rank and class,
Without distinction go to daily Mass,

And pray with fervour to their God most High,
That He would all their daily wants supply,
And lead them on along the narrow road,
That leads to bliss and to His blest abode.
And since the poor have little time to pray,
Who labour for their bread the live-long day,
She teaches them their toils to sanctify,
To raise their hearts to Him who reigns on High,
And when they can, to go upon their knees,
And become members of sodalities;
Whose members join and pray for one another,
And men with leisure help their toiling brother,
And they become like soldiers in the field
Who, strong in numbers, know not how to yield,
And where the strong, the weaker members shield.
And even for those who know not how to read,
The Church has helps to aid them in their need;
Has Beads for those who cannot read or spell
On which they may their pious *Paters* tell,
And *Holy Marys* which they love so well,
And pious pictures speaking to the eye,
To raise their thoughts above the sun and sky;
But heretics, who scarcely pray at all,
May pious pictures superstition call.
Benighted souls, they know not what they say,
And we for them should never cease to pray.
The Catholics, too, the Saints of God invoke,
Who bore themselves the sweet and gentle yoke
Of Jesus Christ, and now with Jesus reign,
And for their clients, graces great obtain.
They can and do for sinners intercede
Before God's throne, and for their clients plead;

For all their friends they great compassion show,
As they our needs and dreadful warfare know.
  True *Education* is a *Means* of grace
Which brings great blessings on the human race.
What Church knows best to educate the child,
Whate'er the disposition, tame or wild?
The Holy Spirit o'er the Church presides,
And in her ruling and her teaching guides;
And hence experience, time's unfailing test,
Has proved her methods to be far the best
To train the intellect with faultless art,
To fill the head, and to improve the heart,
The Christian virtues early to instil,
And bend to righteousness the stubborn will.
Her first great object is the child to train
To virtue bright, the bliss of Heaven to gain;
For what avails all wealth from Pole to Pole
And all the science if you lose your soul?
And learned men are oft the most unwise,
And for a shadow lose the golden prize;
And what avail all science, knowledge, art,
The man who loves not God with all his heart?
Who fears nor God, nor death, nor future pain,
And cares for nought, but sciences profane;
Gives all his time to win a fleeting fame,
And leave behind him but an empty name;
Not that the Church in human matters wise
Doth e'er the human sciences despise,
But, on the contrary, she loves them well,
And wishes all her children to excel
In human sciences, which have their use,
If well employed, and guarded from abuse.

But some apply them not to glorify
The God of science; but to crucify.
Religious handmaids they should ever be,
For truth with truth can never disagree,
Unless for truth we take some fallacy.
    See how the child all other churches train,
Whose zeal is all for sciences profane!
Though for the Bible some great zeal profess,
And seem to love it even to excess.
The Jews once loved the Temple of the Lord,
While they the Temple, not the Lord, adored;
And while the Temple filled their souls with pride,
They loved not Christ; but blindly crucified.
While of the Bible heretics make boast,
They by their morals grieve the Holy Ghost.
They read the Bible, and most glibly quote,
And in their reading never use a note
To guide the judgment of or young or old,
Just as if all its meaning could unfold.
They seem to think the humblest in the land
Can grope his way without a guiding hand,
Though Peter says 'tis hard to understand
Some certain tests in God's own Bible blest,
Which th' unlettered to their ruin wrest.
There's no restriction placed on young or old,
And each one may his own opinion hold;
No judge supreme to guide by right divine,
To tell the sense, or doctrine to define;
And hence the source of all the sects we see,
Who never on a single text agree.
Not so the Church of Rome the truth instils
Into young minds, which she with knowledge fills,

But like the hen that crushes first the grain
Ere she presents it to her chicken train,
She does for youth instruction's food prepare
With zeal, with diligence, and loving care.
She culls instruction from th' inspired page
Which is best suited to their tender age,
And from her Doctors who led holy lives,
And from the Fathers and the Saints derives
The sacred essence of true piety,
Of saving truth, and of morality.
And thus she nourishes the youthful mind
With knowledge, truth, and piety combined,
And while she saves them from a thousand snares,
She for their souls a holy food prepares,
A food preserved from heresy's foul taint,
Which suits the young and helps to make the saint.
And while she gives the nourishment that suits,
She always keeps them from forbidden fruits ;
And hence one source of her great sanctity,
While every sect is but a barren tree,
On which no fruit of holiness is found
Whose trunk is hollow and its roots unsound.

We saw before, and from the Scriptures see,
Christ's Church must *Catholic* for ever be.
What Church but Rome's is such ? can claim
The title *Catholic*, the very name ?
No Church but Rome's can ever hope to trace
Its claim to Catholic as to time and place,
And doctrine too.

It teaches *all* that man doth need to know,
All doctrines taught by Christ so long ago,

Which He commanded to be taught to men,
Till He to judge, returns to earth again.
What other Church is Catholic as to time,
Or half so old, although but in her prime?
All other Churches, contradict who may,
Are young compared, and but of yesterday;
Too late their date, the fact is not denied,
They owed their birth to Royal lust and pride.
If we look o'er the world's great map and trace,
We'll find Rome's Church is Catholic as to place;
That she alone converted all the world,
And from his throne each proud heresiarch hurled;
No matter how great his power, pomp and show,
Her dread anathema soon laid him low.
In vain doth heresy, the child of pride,
Resist her judgment if she once decide,
Though pride corrupts by its unholy leaven
The brightest, greatest, fairest gifts of Heaven,
And next to pride, of vices that disgust
Is blinding, blasting, and degrading lust.

The Church that is on such foundations built,
Can never spread, though much it hide its guilt.
Go now and search the world from east to west
You'll find Rome's Church outnumbers all the rest,
And gaining fast her ancient royal sway
Among the sects now melting to decay
Before the burning rays of truth divine,
As now in England and along the Rhine;
While in America, and other lands,
False Churches wither and the True expands
Her branches wider than in ages past,
O'er rising nations and through regions vast,

Receiving back from every class and grade,
The sons of those who from her bosom strayed,
When Lutheran panthers ravaged all the fold,
Betraying Christ for woman, lust, and gold,
And bartering future joys for present mirth,
And faith divine for fleeting joys of earth.
   And what did Luther, mighty son of Thunder,
But rend the Church of Christendom asunder, }
To ope the way to falsehood and to plunder ?
To rob the people of their faith divine,
To rob the Church of many a holy shrine,
To rob the destitute of daily bread,
The old and hungry, whom the Monks had fed
Without taxation laid on house or land,
But out of charity's o'erflowing hand, }
Which ne'er put on them a disgraceful brand.
   The Church of Rome, which grows and spreads apace,
Can her existence to th' *Apostles* trace,
And show her Popes—two hundred fifty-nine,*
From Peter down in one unbroken line.
This public fact admits of no disguise,
As truthful history amply testifies.
This patent fact no foeman can deny,
Much though he may the Church of Rome decry.
E'en Lord Macaulay, as his writings show
(A brilliant writer, but a bitter foe,
Who hates the Church with such satanic hate,
Yet his admissions do her service great,)
This fact admits, much though he may deplore,
And may her origin divine ignore.

---

* Schouppe.

This writer, viewing from Parnassian slopes,
The long-lived dynasty of Royal Popes,
Looks back—but never wishing to befriend—
And sees this wondrous dynasty extend
To days when Pagan Rome had bent the knee
To Pagan gods in gross idolatry ;
When Pagan Emperors did all they could
To quench the faith of Christ in seas of blood ;
When martyrs were, amid assemblies vast,
To lions, tigers, cameleopards, cast :
So says Macaulay, man of brilliant wit,
Who 'd paint a devil in a Jesuit ;
Who 'd make the Church a seven-headed beast,
And find a demon in a holy Priest.
Yet he admits, while he would fain attack,
The line of Popes to Peter's days goes back,
That th' oldest royal houses we survey
Are youthful all, and but of yesterday,
When with the line of Pontiff Kings compared,
Who ruled the Church, and every peril shared ;
And, arguing from the past, he could not see
That Protestants have any guarantee
That she shall not in vigour live and reign
When London proud, whose navy rules the main,
Shall be, with all its wealth and wondrous trade,
Low laid in ruins and a desert made,
And some New Zealander, 'mid ruined walls,
Shall view to sketch the ruins of St. Paul's.
Can Lord Macaulay or his readers tell,
Where was their Church ere Martin Luther fell ?
A Church begotten of a lustful bed,
And from its birth by crime and rapine fed,
And boasts no other than a royal head.

If by its fruits we're told to judge the tree,
What fruit of Holiness can mortal see
On England's Church, since planted on the soil,
What has she done but plunder and despoil,
Since first she laid her sacrilegious hands
On Rome's old Churches and the Abbey lands;
On sacred vessels made of solid gold,
And everything on which she could lay hold,
T' enrich apostate Priests, and Monkish knaves,
Who were of Royalty the veriest slaves,
And hungry nobles and apostate squires
Of many modern lords the guilty sires.
Those base Apostates bartered faith for gold,
Deceived the people, and religion sold
T' enrich a few and rob an ancient nation
(And this they call a "Glorious Reformation"!)
Of faith divine, God's greatest gift to man,
T' atone for which no earthly riches can.
No doubt Old England has grown rich and great
Since her Church became the creature of the State,
And so were pagan nations in their day;
But who for wealth should throw his soul away?
None but a fool, whatever some may say.
    If marks divine in England's Church we seek,
We find them not—the truth I boldly speak;
And neither do we in the Russo Greek,
Nor any Church, whatever it may be,
That separated from the Holy See.
For whether large such Churches be or small,
From east to west, they're withered branches all;
Since separated from the sacred vine,
They lost all sap and nourishment divine.

The Scriptural *Notes* in Rome's old Church are found,
Whose branches flourish, and whose trunk is sound,
Whose fruits of Sanctity, the world may see
On this divine and Apostolic tree,
Which from the first did flourish and extend
Its healthy branches to the world's end.
In Rome's Old Church, "Immortal milk-white Hind,"
We all the Notes and Marks of Scripture find,
Which prove her Christ's, the only and the True,
Which like the eagle, doth her youth renew,
Which now has lasted nigh two thousand years,
And day by day more vigorous appears.
Of faith divine, she still maintains the fight,
And conquering ever puts her foes to flight;
While human Churches rose at times and fell,
Rome's Church has triumphed o'er the gates of hell;
And proved as clearly as the light of day
Her old foundations never will give way.
She saw the birth of all who quit her side,
How short they flourished, and how soon they died.
Though heresy may live for many a year,
'Tis doomed to die, and dying disappear;
The Church of Christ and of His servants all,
Shall live and flourish till the stars shall fall.

But come and view her trials in the past,
And then confess, she must for ever last,
And see her triumphs over every foe
That sought her ruin and her overthrow,
What she has done since e'er her race began
For fallen nature and the race of man.

END OF PART I.

Part II.

HISTORICAL.

THE Church of Rome, as we have clearly shown,
Of all existing Churches—she alone—
Has all the *Marks* of Christ's own Church sublime,
And she shall flourish till the end of time,
Converting nations, spreading gospel light,
And pointing out the holy way and right
To bliss eternal, and unfading joy,
And all the means her children should employ
To worship God, and every sin detest,
And by that means to gain eternal rest.

But other arguments we have at hand
To make the dullest clearly understand,
That she could not have triumphed o'er her foes
For eighteen centuries, and still oppose
The hosts of hell, in league with all that's base,
Corrupt, and sinful in the human race,
Were she not aided, strengthened, fortified
By Him who for our fallen race had died;
And gave His word, as all the faithful know,
His Church shall triumph over every foe.

Let us then, reader, and as best we can,
The Church's *trials* and her *triumphs* scan,
And you'll conclude, as I indeed opine,
The Church of Rome's unfailing and divine.

What was the world, and what the race of man
When Rome's old Church her mission great began ?

'Twas Pagan all, idolatrous and dark;
Its gods were idols, I may here remark.
Its vices dark were by its laws unchecked,
Its hateful crimes in robes of honour decked:
Its grossest sins excited nought of shame,
E'en though so frightful that we cannot name !
The Church of God alone, of God Most High,
Could hope to cure the world and purify.
But see the task she had to undertake
For God, for Christ, and for her children's sake !
And see how weak she was to human sight,
For such a stubborn, such a deadly fight;
How great her victories, as well appears,
From her long life of nigh two thousand years;
So full of conquests in the ages past,
So great, so mighty, permanent and vast,
That none save fools shall dare presume to say,
She shall not last till earth shall pass away.
When she appeared, the world, save Jews alone,
Fell down and worshipped gods of stick and stone;
And of the Jews 'tis only some embrace
The faith of Christ, and seek His saving grace.
  See how the Pagans to their idols clung,
Erected temples, and the praises sung
Of gods and goddesses, whose passions base
Were sad examples to the human race;
And gave encouragement to passions strong,
And boldly sanctioned every sin and wrong;
No virtue practised or by great or small,
And vice and wickedness were all in all.
The greatest vices were as virtues prized,
And by religion sanctioned—authorized !

The greatest drunkard honoured Bacchus most,
And to be drunk was then a pious boast!
To honour Venus (word of evil fame)
By prostitution did but honour claim!
And yet no fire from outraged heaven fell
On Pagan Rome—the vestibule of hell!
With all its vice 'twas destined still to be
The future home of Peter's Holy See;
And from the depth of its corruption base,
To show the power of sanctifying grace.
Nor theft nor robbery were ever cloaked,
And thieves and robbers Mercury invoked;
Laverna also was invoked to bless
Both thieves and robbers and to grant success!
  The Pagan worship dazzled Pagan eyes,
Which to its gods saw gorgeous temples rise.
Their priests were richly, nay, superbly clad,
The wealthy gave the richest gifts they had;
The victims sacrificed were richly decked,
(To wealth and pomp the Pagans paid respect,)
Emperors, Consuls, bearing emblems bright,
Add pomp and splendour to the sacred rite,
And in the worship thousands took delight.
And after public sacrifices grand,
Went feasting, balls, and banquets hand in hand;
And dances, games, and gladiatorial fights,
Which gave the Romans such unfeigned delights.
Such was the Pagan worship in those days,
When th' infant Church began her head to raise,
To cast her net for souls, and draw them in
From out a world of wickedness and sin.
In Pagan worship we but grossness find,
Yet it gave pleasure to the Pagan mind.

The Pagans thought that to their gods they owed
Their health, their wealth, and every gift bestowed;
In war their triumphs, and their bliss in peace,
All cures in sickness, and from pain release;
And hence to idols they devoutly cling,
Adorn their temples, and their praises sing.
Such was indeed the Pagan world at large,
When Christ gave Peter th' important charge,
The Pagan world from darkness to reclaim,
To preach His Gospel, and make known His Name;
To fear not man, nor Satan, King of Pride,
As He would ever with His Church abide.
   If men would know how great the fight must be,
Just look at Rome where Peter fixed his See;
Where Satan long had fixed his ebon throne,
And made the city and the earth his own !
O Pagan Rome, the sink of every sin,
To paint thy vices how shall I begin ?
But here I must my hasty words recall,
Nor saint nor angel could recount them all;
'Tis only devils from the depths of hell
That could their number and their malice tell !
What then was Rome when Peter came to preach,
Whose depth of guilt no mortal eye could reach ?
To human sight how fearful were the odds,
Four hundred temples,* thirty thousand gods !
Unnumbered wealth, red seas of sin and guilt,
And no recounting all the blood she spilt.
Her dread religion one of sin and hate,
And cruelty that nought could satiate.

---

* Some put the number at 270.

Her morals too, if we examine close,
Were shameful, horrid, infamously gross;
Her very temples, so superbly built,
Were schools of lust, debauchery, and guilt!
Her feasts were hot-beds of the grossest vice,
Of nameless sins—but let those words suffice.
Her gods, inventions of men's lust and pride,
Were all the grosser passions deified;
And gave a sanction—were a sanction sought—
To wicked laws with every evil fraught,
And every sin as dark as hell and night,
Whose very mention fills us with affright.

What were the *laws* of Rome, or were they wise,
Or did they aid her sons to civilize,
Or served they not to blind and brutalize?
Her laws were laws of cruelty and hate,
As may be seen from what I shall narrate.
The *daughter* was the brutal father's slave,
Whom he might sell ere he in marriage gave;
And then the husband had the power to sell,
Or to dismiss her, as historians tell.
Divorce was lawful without moral cause,
Nor did religion once oppose the laws.
The helpless *child* could by the laws be killed
Before its birth, just as the parents willed;
And after birth, when cruel laws required,
And wicked rites, which hell itself inspired,
To offer victims and select the child
For sacrifice to idols so defiled!
Poor *slaves* as chattels were then bought and sold,
While their harsh treatment makes the blood run cold;
Chained down like beasts—a sad and direful lot—
And branded all with irons burning hot;

At night imprisoned in some dungeon dread,
And lashed like animals, but far worse fed;
And put to death for faults by no means grave,
(For slight mistakes a lady killed her slave,)
And many a slave did oft a victim fall
To slightest things which were not faults at all.
If a man was murdered, all his guiltless slaves
Were put to death and sent to early graves,
Although quite free from murder or from strife,
And would have died to save their master's life !
    Prisoners of war—an awful, dreadful doom—
Were sacrificed upon the conqueror's tomb,
Or sold to slavery and dreadful woes,
Or kept to fight in gladiatorial shows
For the amusement of the ruder mind,
And of the polished, wealthy, and refined,
For high and low by cruelty made blind !
Ah, such was Rome, and such her cruel laws,
When Peter came to plead the Christian cause.
And who was Peter in the Pagans' eyes,
And his meek helpers in their enterprise,
The greatest ever since the world began,
Yet undertaken for the good of man ?
And what did those Apostles poor require
Of men deep sunk in sin's unholy mire,
And yet so full of wealth, of pomp and pride,
They could not humble poverty abide,
Much less correction and severe reproof
From men from whom they ever held aloof ?
And who are those poor fishermen who came
This proud voluptuous city to reclaim ?
Which conquered earth, and made the world obey
Its laws imperial and confess its sway ?

To ask earth's queen idolatry to spurn,
Her idols old to cast away and burn ?
To share her wealth with those she hated most
To hate these things that were her pride and boast ?
To mortify the sinful flesh, and flee
All dreadful sins of vile impurity,
And all the pleasures which her children prize,
E'en though offensive to a Christian's eyes ;
T' obey the followers of One who died
A shameful death, condemned and crucified !
And to do penance hard to flesh and blood,
For what to them appeared a future good !
And this it is those strangers came to seek,
Those humble Fishermen so poor and meek,
And so deficient in the Pagan eye
Of all that 's lofty, noble, great and high—
Genius, eloquence, exalted rank,
Riches, titles, power—all which sank
Before the preaching of unlettered men,
So weak, so powerless, to human ken !
  And who is it that doth these men inspire ?
The Holy Ghost who sat in tongues of fire
Upon their feeble heads, and made them feel
A strength divine, a bold and burning zeal,
To preach the faith of Christ to young and old,
With ardour burning and as lions bold :—
To preach the Gospel, and its truth unfold
To Jew and Gentile—to the nations all,
And rescue them from Satan's cruel thrall,
And free the victims he in fetters bound
Of sin, and guilt, and ignorance profound
Of that great God who has created all
The heavens above, and this our earthly ball.

And they went forth and preached from east to west,
And north and south the heavenly Gospel blest;
And Paul's Epistles tell with what success,
Till million converts praise the Lord and bless.
From him we learn Christ's banner was unfurled
O'er Pagan Rome, the mistress of the world:
For blessed Paul, the reader here may note,
A great Epistle to the Romans wrote
In which he praises their great faith so pure,
So filled with zeal and certain to endure,
Where blessed Peter set hell's captives free,
And where he fixed his everlasting See.
    And did the Fishermen at length succeed
To wean from luxury and love of greed—
From wealth, indulgence, and the pomp of pride,
Men so corrupt—and get them to divide
Their wealth 'mong those whom they were taught to hate,
And ask themselves to change their lives and state,
To part with all their wealth, and to embrace
What they regarded objects of disgrace—
Meekness, poverty, contempt, and scorn,
The portions of the poor and lowly born?
Can all their luxury supplanted be
By patience, **penance, meekness, poverty?**
Can it be hoped that Rome will set aside
Her wealth, **her wantonness,** and wicked pride,
To clothe herself in ashes and in weeds,
And to do penance for her wicked deeds;
To fast, abstain, **to suffer want and cold,**
As some atonement for her vices old?
    Yes, Peter **conquered, but at what a cost!**
Of seas of blood, through which the martyrs crossed

Unto eternity with Him to reign,
For whom to die is everlasting gain
Of bliss and glory which no words can paint,
Nor heart of man conceive—nor greatest saint,
Or holy Doctor, skilled in learnèd lore—
Nor human vision can their depths explore!
St. Peter and St. Paul of boundless zeal
Pour forth their blood, their faith divine to seal;
And onward still the blood of martyrs flows
For three long centuries of dismal woes!
The cruel Pagans made the faithful die
For serving Him who made the earth and sky;
And hell was troubled, of the Church afraid,
And the conversions the Apostles made,
And moved the Emperors, and men of might
To rage and hate against the Gospel light,
Which shone and spread before the people's eyes,
Which made the converts Pagan gods despise,
And break the idols they had loved so well,
And cast them off as instruments of hell;
And quit the pleasures they so dearly prized,
And lead such lives as holy men advised;
To labour, hunger, suffer heat and cold,
And part with all their riches and their gold;
And for their old religion to embrace,
That of a member of the Jewish race,
Whom to be God the Jews themselves denied,
And whom as guilty, Pilate crucified!
    And now, dear reader, let us cast our eyes
O'er all the Persecutions as they rise,
To shed the blood of martyrs—causing tears—
To fall in floods for full three hundred years;

And view the noble martyrs who withstood
The rage of tyrants who had shed the blood
Of million martyrs—as we read eleven—
And sent those millions to the bliss of heaven;
While other millions, as old writers tell,
Had with the dead in Catacombs to dwell,
To keep the lamp of faith still burning bright
During Persecution's dismal night;
Till freedom's dawn shot forth its cheering ray,
And all could openly adore and pray.

   Poor infant Church, how weak you were and frail,
When first arose the fierce and dreadful gale
Of persecution, nothing could withstand,
Unless supported by th' Almighty Hand
Of God Omnipotent, who brings to nought
The power of tyrants 'mid the evils wrought
Among His servants, who are doomed to die,
And by their blood their faith to testify
In Jesus Christ who reigns in bliss above,
And died for them to prove His boundless love.

   And who, I ask, the evil work began,
When through old Rome the blood of martyrs ran
Along the streets, along the public road,
And in the Circus like a river flowed
To glut the tyranny, and satiate
A brutal monster's savage, cruel hate?
A man who centred in his person base
The greatest vices of the human race.
He did his nights with vile companions spend,
And of his wickedness there was no end.
He poisoned his greatest benefactor's son,
And ever gloried in the evil done.

He killed his mother, and he killed his wife,
Deprived his tutor, Seneca, of life;
Set fire to Rome, which burned for eight long days,
His only object to enjoy the blaze !
And on the pious Christians cast the blame,
Their Pagan foes to madden and inflame !
The Christians then were seized—e'en holy priests—
And covered with the skins of savage beasts
For wicked dogs to torture and devour ;
And all could witness faith's triumphant power.
And some were covered o'er with pitch and wax,
(Strange modes of torture tyrant never lacks),
And some were tied to posts as lamps to light,
And give to NERO and his friends delight.
'Twas in this reign, a reign of blood and pride,
That great St. Paul and blessed Peter died—
The one beheaded—the other crucified ;
'Twas under Nero those great pillars fell,
And by their deaths o'ercame the powers of hell,
And taught the world 'tis useless to assail
The Church of Christ, though seeming weak and frail,
Since 'gainst that Church hell's gates cannot prevail.
The blood of martyrs makes the Church more strong,
While earth and hell her trials great prolong ;
And tyrants all of persecuting zeal
Are made in time the wrath of God to feel ;
And so was Nero, who was doomed to see
A wretched end at th' age of thirty-three !
    DOMITIAN, too, who for a god would pass,
Persecuted with a heart of brass ;
And e'en his relatives of noble rank,
Whose blood with eagerness the tigers drank.

D

This cruel fool, as cruel as unwise,
Spent many days in catching, killing flies;
Ah! would he killed but flies, and let alone
Flavius Clemens and the great St. John,
And thousand others whom he tortured, killed,
And Heaven only knows what blood he spilled.

The cruel work to wicked TRAJAN passed,
Who had Ignatius to the lions cast—
Ignatius brave, disciple of St. John,
The noblest soul, the lions seized upon,
Who ruled for forty years the ancient See
Of Antioch, and judged himself to be
"The wheat of Christ," desirous to be ground
By wicked beasts, and yearning to be found
"The Bread of Christ;" and so he was indeed;
Two lions tore him, and devoured with speed
Before a multitude of Pagan eyes,
Of those who clapped and uttered joyous cries;
But St. Ignatius passes to a throne
Where sighs, and tears, and sorrows are unknown.

At intervals the Saints enjoyed repose,
And soon again a tempest wild arose,
And swept the empire with terrific force,
Slaying thousands in its dreadful course.
The number slain is known to God alone,
And those around His everlasting throne,
Where all the martyrs wear a brilliant crown
Of bliss and joy, of glory and renown.
But human tongue and human pen would fail
Their numbers and their sufferings to retail;
And in my narrative, I only name
A few deserving of immortal fame.

Not only Rome, but through her empire wide
Were cities, towns, and public places dyed
With martyrs' blood, and Egypt, ancient Gaul,
And Africa saw countless martyrs fall,
And giving proof of bravery of soul
As they faced death and reached the dreaded goal.
Under ADRIAN Symphorosa died,
Of th' early Church the glory and the pride.
Her husband—officer, and tribune both—
Laid down his life for Christ, and nothing loth,
His noble lady braved the tyrant's ire,
And did, brave soul, to martyrdom aspire,
And sought to be among the martyred ones,
And to lead with her all her seven sons;
And so she did, and filled their souls with zeal
Till all the seven were broken on the wheel,
And she into the Anio was cast,
And thence her soul to Heaven's glory passed.
Though brief my narrative, I must not pass
The noble martyr, Saint Felicitas.
A lady, too, of noble birth and high,
But yet more noble by her constancy.
The Pagan Priests had often made complaints
To ANTONINUS of the Christian Saints,
And named the widow St. Felicitas,
Whose faith was firm as a wall of brass,
Who worshipped God alone in bliss enthroned,
And Pagan gods and goddesses disowned;
And to her seven sons she points on high
And asks them view the bright and starry sky,
Where Jesus Christ awaits with golden crowns
The soldiers true, who brave the tyrant's frowns,

And all the evils he can do and dare,
And all the torture he can make them share;
And bids them die for Christ who died for all,
And shall to glory all His martyrs call;
And so they died for Him, the noble seven,
And with their mother winged their flight to heaven.
But not in Rome alone the war was waged,
Throughout the empire wicked men engaged
In wicked efforts to exterminate
The Christians all as hostile to the State.
'Tis now in Smyrna persecution dread
Doth raise full high its fierce and brazen head.
AURELIUS, skilled in philosophic lore,
And his Proconsul drunk with human gore,
Tortured poor Christians in a thousand ways,
Whose crime it was to sing their Maker's praise;
And some were burned, and some by beasts devoured,
Some torn by whips; and men, by laws empowered,
Laid all their bones and very entrails bare,
Nor child, nor mother, did the monsters spare!
Yet thousands flocked (so great the power of grace)
To look for death, and torments to embrace.
No sort of torture had been left untried,
And yet the martyrs neither groaned nor sighed;
But suffered meekly as our Lord had done,
And nobly thus the crown of glory won.
The love of death so much among them grew,
A youth, Germanicus, with ardour flew
To meet the lions; and the Pagan crowd
Were so provoked they shouted long and loud,
And said, "Away with him (who freely sought
This death), and let old Polycarp be brought."

And so he was, that glorious old man,
And the Proconsul thus his speech began :—
"Respect thy hairs, by Cæsar swear and say,
I'll banish all the impious away.
Blaspheme thy God, and I shall thee discharge,
Release thee from thy fetters, and enlarge."
And Smyrna's bishop, Polycarp, replied :—
"Shall I blaspheme my Saviour who has died
For me and for th' entire human race,
And has prepared for me in Heaven a place,
And joys ineffable, and endless bliss,
If I am valiant in a war like this ?
I've served him long, for fourscore years and six,
And then shall I, when on this Cross I fix
My weeping eyes, blaspheme His Holy Name,
Who died for me a painful death, and shame
The faithful flock I long have taught to give
Their lives for Him that they with Him may live ?
From Him I have received but blessings great,
And shall I then one moment hesitate
To give my life for Him—a poor return,
Although you may my body cut and burn ?"
"But Sir, remember, I the beasts can call,
Whose very presence doth the brave appall,
And I can, too, the flaming torch apply,
And make the enemies of Cæsar die."
"Then call your beasts, which you have near at hand;
Or, if you wish, apply the burning brand,
But do not hope my faith in Christ to shake,
For I rejoice to suffer for His sake.
While Christians are to God Almighty true,
They wrong not Cæsar, but give him his due,

And if he will pursue with vengeful ire,
'Twill save us all from everlasting fire."
His death they earnestly demand, and strive
To have the holy martyr burned alive,
The light of Asia, and the Christian's joy,
Who did his best all idols to destroy.
The aged martyr stood the stake beside,
His holy hands behind him firmly tied,
And raising up to Heaven his loving eyes,
He sends before him ardent prayers and sighs—
The pile is lighted, and the martyr dies,
And flies to heaven and to eternal rest,
Having nobly thus the Faith of Christ professed.
   'Twas in this reign that Justin Martyr died,
The great Apologist, who justified
The Christians in their constancy; who owed
To God their lives, and all He had bestowed;
To whom they owe all homage, worship, praise,
To whom they owe their hearts, and thoughts to raise,
To keep His law and fly the thoughts of sin,
That they may all a crown of glory win
From Him, who made the earth, the sun, the sky,
And shall reward His servants all on high.
He by his pen defends the Saints, and shows
The Christian converts never were the foes
Of Cæsar, or his kingdom, and are true
In their allegiance, and the homage due
The temporal head and ruler of the State,
And yet receive but punishment and hate !
But yet flows on the persecuting tide,
And led to death, St. Justin nobly died ;
And having won on earth a bright renown,
Ascends to Heaven, and wears the martyr's crown.

After short respite persecution's flame
Breaks out again against the Christian name.
Hell finds its agents dark to fan the fire,
And light again the Pagan's vengeful ire,
By infamous stories, base invented lies,
And every plot the wicked can devise.
They say that Christians acted like the beast,
And that they did on slaughtered infants feast.
Such were the stories which they spread in Gaul—
At Lyons where those tortures dread appall
The stoutest hearts, when nought but grace on high
Could brace their hearts to suffer and to die.
Some were drawn and stretched upon the rack;
Others had heated plates on sides and back
To burn the flesh unto the very bone,
And others were to bulls and tigers thrown;
And some in red-hot chairs were forced to sit,
Who never did a single fault commit.
Blandina, a servant maid, beyond the rest
Great courage showed and Jesus Christ confessed,
And died heroically a martyr blest.
And yet the Christians daily multiplied,
And much provoked the cruel Pagan's pride,
Still persecution through the empire spread,
And filled the land with terror and with dread.
    And now the direful tempest fierce and fast,
From Gallic Lyons unto Carthage passed.
At first SEVERUS seemed not much inclined
To heed the Christians, nay, to them was kind;
But on a sudden—no apparent cause—
He published edicts—sanguinary laws—
And persecution waved its wicked lance
In Egypt, Africa, and ancient France.

In Egypt rolled the desolating wave
O'er thousands martyred, faithful, true and brave, }
And bravest of them all a female slave,
By nature beautiful, and virtue rich, •
Named Potamiana, who in boiling pitch
Suffered three hours of agonizing pain,
For which she now enjoys a blissful reign
Of bliss and glory in that kingdom bright,
Where angels dwell in beatific light.
   In Lyons once again the tempest rose,
Which troops surround and deal their deadly blows,
And butchered nineteen thousand—not to speak
Of women, children, feeble ones and weak,
And 'mid those saints, the pride and boast of Gaul,
Was Irenæus, greatest of them all.
And now to Carthage spread the dreadful flame
Of persecution 'gainst the Christian name.
There many martyrs did to glory pass;
Perpetua brave and Saint Felicitas
Do more especially attention claim,
As both inherit everlasting fame.
The first was noble, married, and caressed
A tender infant clinging to her breast;
The second was, brave soul, eight months with child
(But this moved not her persecutors wild).
The harsh unfeeling judge condemned them both—
Their sad condition made him nothing loth—
They were confined in prison till the day
They were to die—to wicked beasts a prey.
The Christians prayed Felicitas might see
Her infant born before she ceased to be,
And so she did, but yet not love of child,
Nor tears, nor prayers of a parent mild,

Could shake her firm resolve for Christ to die,
Her faith in Him to show and testify.
 'Twould tire my reader, and fatigue my pen,
To go through all the Persecutions ten
Through which the Church, the first three hundred years,
'Mid seas of blood, and floods of briny tears,
Had lived and struggled, toiled, and bore the light
Of Gospel truth all through the Pagan night,
Till God was pleased to humble all her foes,
To crown her triumphs, and to grant repose.
From what I have in simple numbers said,
And truthfully, of persecutions dread
(I've nothing said to strictness still inclined,
The reader won't in ancient Authors find),
The reader may infer how bloody, base,
Were all the persecutions that took place
Under MAXIMINIAN, DECIUS, DIOCLESIAN dread;
The numbers killed, the blood of martyrs shed.
And while these persecutions great appall,
Dioclesian's was the worst of all;
It raged with greatest fury in the East,
And did on plunder and oppression feast,
And on the thousands driven to be slain,
Through love of cruelty and cursèd gain.
The Christians all were driven to submit
To every torture which their foes thought fit
T' inflict on every Christian young and old,
On whom they could for punishment lay hold.
Whole towns were burned, and not a soul could flee
From torments dread, and awful butchery.
Some had the flesh scraped from their bones till dead,
And some were killed by pouring boiling lead

Into their wounds; some slashed from head to foot,
And salt and pepper in their gashes put!
And some were roasted on a raging fire
Till they in agony of pain expire.
Who can depict their tortures? who can tell
How much they suffered from the rage of hell,
Which saw its filthy idols overthrown,
And God and all His attributes made known?
And from a world so long in darkness sunk,
And made by pride and hateful passions drunk;
And coming round the demon to dethrone,
And worship God, and worship Him alone.
What wonder hell with spite and rage should burn
To see its worshippers from idols turn,
And from the slavery of pride and lust,
And fast becoming humble, chaste, and just!

I must not longer on such pictures dwell,
Though I should like of other Saints to tell;
But those great Saints are so well known to fame,
I give their history when I give their name.
Such is St. Lawrence whom the Pagans roast,
And Agnes chaste, the early Church's boast.
The Church in which those noble martyrs died
Is Rome's old Church—the ever true and tried.

In Dioclesian's reign the earth was red
With all the streams of martyrs' blood he shed,
Until he thought (old pillars tell the same),
He blotted out the very Christian name.
Those marble pillars still exist in Spain,
All bearing witness to his cruel reign;
But God avenged the cruel tyrant's guilt,
For all the blood of holy martyrs spilt.

But did the Christians find no able pen
To plead the cause of deeply injured men,
Thus made to suffer for no crime at all,
Those tortures dread that frighten and appall?
Ah, yes they did, as they have ever found
Champions great of intellect profound,
Of learning, eloquence, and burning zeal,
Who'd face the lions and the burnished steel
To show their faith—the faithful to defend,
To preach Christ crucified, and to extend
His blessed teaching, and to bring to nought
All Pagan worship with such evils fraught.
Of those great champions I've already named
St. Justin Martyr; but Tertullian famed,
And Origen—Apologist renowned—
Whom fame immortal has for ever crowned,
I must not pass without a word of praise,
In these my simple, unambitious lays.
Tertullian, learned priest of Carthage, wrote
His great Apology which critics vote
The ablest, best, most eloquent defence
Of·Christian teaching, morals, innocence.
He pleaded well the early Christian cause,
And showed how impious were the Pagan laws;
How loathsome were its worship, and its rites,
And how indecent were its public sights;
He shows how grand the holy Christian creed,
And how adapted to man's every need;
How it exalts, ennobles, and refines,
And every virtue in the heart enshrines,
While every vice it plucks and flings away,
Like noxious weeds, to wither and decay;

How it renews and renovates the earth,
And sows the seeds of an immortal birth;
And raises man when this short life is flown,
To reign with God and share a blissful throne.
  Origen, too, for erudition famed,
And genius, eloquence—though often blamed
For strange opinions which, alas! he held,
As did Tertullian, who like him excelled;
But faults apart, he fought a noble fight
With Pagan giants, men of wondrous might,
And did the greatest of them all confound,
A man of skill, and arguments unsound,
The crafty, subtle Celsus, who would blind
By skilful fallacies, the keenest mind;
But truth gave strength to Origen's right hand,
Which laid Goliah rolling in the sand,
For error never can the truth withstand;
Though both with equal skill and art advance,
Victorious truth shall wield its victor lance.
  And now at length dread persecution ends,
And Royal Heads become the Church's friends,
And first and greatest of this royal line,
Raised up by God, was noble Constantine,
Surnamed the Great, the Church's wounds to heal,
And to support her in her ardent zeal
To spread the Gospel, fallen man to raise
From error dark, and error's sinful ways.
But we have not one-half her trials told,
Ere Constantine protects the Christian fold;
For, during persecution's dismal night,
The Church of God had other foes to fight
Than Pagans rude, who felt a savage joy
The Christian fold to ravage and destroy,

And far more subtle in their hate and guile,
Though not so bloody, brutal, base, and vile;
More poisonous too, as more imbued with pride,
More hard to conquer, since they lurk inside,
In league with enemies that make a rout,
Attack her walls, and ramparts from without,
While those vile traitors would give up the keys,
And those internal foes are heresies.
    Rank heresy has been, and e'er shall be,
The Church's greatest, subtlest enemy,
Since heresy is first-born child of pride,
With Satan ever and his hosts allied.
Since Adam fell (the devil's first recruit)—
The bounty offered was forbidden fruit—
Our race is prone to covet, taste, and see
The blooming fruit of some forbidden tree.
A tree of knowledge is a tree of fame,
And good or bad, men wish to get a name.
God-given knowledge is a gift divine,
But men more often to the bad incline.
The love of fame, though some may deem it wrong,
If once a passion is exceeding strong,
And good men, too, will often wish to know
Things not expedient, and will often go
Beyond poor reason's depth, and seek to find
Things not attainable by human mind,
(And all to leave a hollow fame behind.)
Human reason, bright though be its eye,
Without Faith's light that cometh from on high,
And giving light by which we may discern
Those truths divine he could not elsewhere learn,
Regarding God, a Being infinite;
Regarding man, how he may serve aright;

Regarding evils which afflict him sore,
And their dark source which he would fain explore
By Reason's light, which all who think must know,
Is now as weak as centuries ago,
When great philosophers pursued its light,
And ne'er emerged from darkness and from night.
They could not solve life's problem nor succeed,
Which shows of faith poor reason stands in need,
To know God's truth, or e'en the plainest things,
No matter how it prunes its tiny wings;
And faith itself to cast its brilliant flame
Must be the true, and not a faith in name.
Hence false religions oft pretences make,
That men from them should all instructions take,
And light, and guidance, on the way to go
To bliss on high, and shun the pains below.
And since fallacious arguments do blind,
Strong doubts will sometimes seize an honest mind,
And hence to question every man is prone,
And victory rests with simple faith alone,
Which pleases God, who gives the help we need,
When men with humble hearts accept the creed,
And put all idle, curious thoughts away,
And hear the Church, and lovingly obey:
For God has given His holy Church to guide
Poor fallen man, for whom His Son had died,
But all is lost, if men are led by pride.
    And so were led some philosophic Jews,
Who joined the Church of Christ, and still refuse
(By pride and foolish thinking led astray)
The Church of Christ in all things to obey;
And such were also learnèd Gentiles too,
Who sought to blend old doctrines with the new,

And, as knowledge puffeth up, they thought,
They to the Church some great advantage brought,
And that their talents, and their knowledge vain
Were to the Church a great and mighty gain ;
And hence their wounded pride, and bitter spite,
When she condemned their errors dark as night.
From these reflections every reader sees
What foes to truth were ancient heresies.
  While we those heresies awhile pursue,
Let's read the Church's wondrous triumphs too,
And viewing the Church in beauty of design,
We must confess Rome's Church to be divine.
No Church that is not, could so live and last,
For eighteen centuries—a lengthened past—
And be so vigorous, and full of life,
While earth and hell excite religious strife,
And war against the Church, they hate and dread,
And 'gainst Christ's Vicar, its anointed Head.
Let us look back upon the Church, and trace
The blessings shed upon the human race
By her exalted missionary zeal,
Which brings rich blessings on the common weal,
Since first St. Peter in the temple preached,
And since the words of Paul the Gentiles reached ;
What she has done all darkness to dispel,
And put to flight the raging hosts of hell ;
To civilize the lawless race of man,
And give him freedom when and where she can,
And educate him not for earth alone,
But for a future kingdom and a throne.
She for the truth maintained a noble fight,
And put her foes, the heretics, to flight ;

Preserved the faith without the slightest taint,
And sent to Heaven many a blessèd Saint.
What other Church has sent a single one,
Or ever shall as long as time shall run?

Since foes assail her, in rebellion rise,
Deny her doctrine, and her words despise,
Resist her power, and the truth gainsay,
And tempt her children from the fold to stray,
Christ gave her power to punish, and repel
Th' attacks of all who murmur and rebel;
To cut them off, to wither and to rot,
Till in the end they share the demon's lot,
If pertinacious in their sin and pride,
Rejecting still the truths they first denied.
Who but the Church of Rome could meet such foes,
Could foil their efforts, and return their blows?
And every day that passes o'er her head,
She has to meet and conquer foemen dread,
And lay them sprawling prostrate at her feet,
And so she gains a victory complete.

Just look at England at the present day,
And her rich prelates—learnèd men they say—
What do they do to answer and confound
The monstrous errors spread her shores around?
Where is their strength, their courage, and their zeal?
But, ah, perhaps, their want of power—they feel!
To war with error they unwilling seem,   ⎫
The Privy Council being Judge supreme,   ⎬
And silence wise the better course they deem. ⎭
And so Agnostics wildest errors spread,   ⎫
Nor Church, nor Bishop do they seem to dread, ⎬
If Church we call, which owns the Queen as head. ⎭

The tide is rising, and I greatly fear,
This English Church will shortly disappear,
And leave behind it not a single trace
Of Christian dogma or redeeming grace ;
Except the ancient Church extend its roots,
Now, nourished well by those called *"Rome's Recruits."*
She is extending, and extending well,
As that same volume *"Rome's Recruits"* can tell.
I'm glad to say this book has changed its name,
If not through love at least through honest shame—
May Heaven to her another Austin send ;
But I must now this short digression end.

The roaring demons never sleep we know,
And hence the Church is ne'er without a foe—
Some leading error soon to pass away,
Or some new heresy to lead astray.
None but the Church of Christ could overthrow
The hosts of Satan, as false Churches know.
'Tis she has crushed all heresies that rose
'Gainst her authority, and dared oppose
Her power to rule, authority to teach,
And to condemn when men foul errors preach,
That would the faith destroy or morals blight,
And rob the world of pure religious light,
Involving earth in darkness and in night.

Ere the first century had reached its close,
Bold teachers of dark heresy arose,
And false Messiahs who denied the true,
And into error many Christians drew.
Then followed wicked Gnostics who denied
That Christ was God or that a Man-God died !
Long were the tale, and hard in verse to tell,
One-half the errors into which they fell,

Which tried the Church, and caused her many tears,
And many pangs for full six hundred years.
To tell one-half would volumes large require,
Fatigue the writer, and the reader tire.
To tell what errors wicked Arius taught,
What dreadful evils proud Sabellius wrought,
What errors dread Pelagius did embrace
Upon the all-important subject—grace.
But notwithstanding all the pride and lies
Of wicked men who fain would pass for wise,
Would plant dissension, and would sow the seed
Of poisonous error, and destroy the creed,
The Church held forth the torch of truth divine
T' enlighten all who worshipped at her shrine;
And drove the heretics, an impious race,
Those wolves of error, to their hiding-place,
Who by the lightning of her censures fell,
The shame of Christians, and the sport of hell.
For sake of unity, though much she prized,
One jot of truth she never compromised,
(For unity is but a rope of sand,
If truth and error should go hand in hand;
As they must e'er in erring churches go,
Whose flocks are left to wander to and fro),
And never shall, until the stars shall fall,
Admit one error, howsoever small,
As do the heretics, and ruin all.
  Whoever follows the historic page
Will find Rome's Church in each succeeding age
Condemning heresy with all her might,
And holding high truth's blazing banner bright.
Let tongues condemn her—e'en the tongues of kings
And every weapon king or tyrant flings

At her authority, she judges all
Who dare her judgment into question call.
Not so false churches wanting Heaven's aid,
Which always are of haughty men afraid,
And compromise the truth, and basely yield,
And leave the foeman master of the field.
Whatever dogma heretics can show
Soon melts away just like the winter snow,
(Not dogmas, but opinions do they hold,
For dogmas are for those within the fold.)
Truth mixed with error never stands the test,
And is a useless mixture at the best.
No church of heretics can e'er define
The truth for cleric, layman, or divine;
But leaves the Bible in the people's hands,
Not caring who it is that understands
The text he reads without a note or gloss,
Or whether reading be a gain or loss;
But he who steers without a chart or guide,
But private judgment, flounders in the tide.
  The Church still triumphed as she triumphs now,
And triumphs shall for ever deck her brow.
She crushed the Donatists and Manichees,
And many other wicked heresies,
Who in her early days, so great their pride,
Religion's fundamental truths denied;
Those truths essential for the flock to hold,
To save their souls and keep within the fold,
Where richest graces are dispensed to all
Who hold the faith of Peter and of Paul,
That is of Christ, for they His footsteps trod,
Fulfilled all justice, and now reign with God.

Now almost every early heresy
Erred on the dogma of the Trinity,
And th' Incarnation,—mysteries indeed,
The strong foundation of the Christian creed,
Which take away, there's nothing left to save,
And hell would soon again the world enslave.
Pelagius held, though Adam never fell,
He still should die, and bid to life farewell,
And that his sin, though great indeed it be,
Had never stained his numerous progeny!
That th' unbaptized enjoy eternal life,
And none need grace though great man's war and strife;
And to this teaching may the reader trace
A host of errors on the subject—grace.

   Nestorius, favourite of the Evil One,
Held Christ was only God's adopted Son.
This rebel worst since heresy began,
This impious, vain, and proud, ambitious man
Declared that Christ was not divine at all,
That men should not the Blessed Virgin call
God's Mother, since her Son was not divine,
But only Man, and one of Adam's line;
Such horrid blasphemies amazed the world,
Which at its author divers curses hurled.

   Eutyches held, a doctrine very sad,
That Christ Our Lord no real body had.

   The *Donatists* held—themselves to evil prone—
Christ's Church consisted of the just alone;
That if a sinner should in sin baptize,
The act's invalid, and no grace supplies.
But why recount the various errors held
By all the heretics, that had rebelled

Against the Church while she was in her youth,
Maintaining, guarding God's eternal truth ?
Their name is legion, but they passed away,
As shall all others of the present day ;
But God's own Church in strength and beauty grows,
And shall for ever on her rock repose.
Nor wind, nor tide shall e'er remove a stone,
Till Christ in judgment sits upon His throne,
And all the heresies like tares are bound,
And cast in bundles into hell profound,
While true believers are in glory crowned.
But God raised up a host of champions great,
To defend the Church's cause, and state
Her case with eloquence and wondrous force
Of argument, which in its course
Swept errors, fallacies, and lies aside,
(So great the force of truth's pellucid tide,)
Like rotten weeds upon the ocean wave,
While Peter's barque ne'er lost a single stave,
By all th' attacks of Satan's pirate crews,
Or Pagan tyrant, oft though he imbrues
In martyrs' blood his crime-polluted hands,
The Church still triumphs, and for ever stands.
    Some from within, some from without, assail,
But all in vain as neither could prevail.
God gave her champions to defend the right,
To combat error, and to spread the light,
And scatter to the sporting winds of heaven
The fallacies of heresy and the leaven ;
And proving that the children who rebel,
Are nothing but emissaries of hell ;

That all men should the traitor vile detest,
Who aims a dagger at his Mother's breast,
And would through lust, or avarice, or pride,
The seamless garment of our Lord divide.
Her brave defenders all their blows repell'd,
And at defiance her assailants held.
One convert then the prophet's words recalls,
"The children of strangers shall build up thy walls;"
Aye, Justin Martyr came to see the light,
And, boldly armed for the sacred fight,
Refuted Tryphon, and most clearly showed
How much the world to her teaching owed.
And later on great Doctors of renown
Were then raised up the holy work to crown,
To defend the truth, and noble words to speak;
Some wrote in Latin, some in Classic Greek.
And of the latter, Athanasius great
O'erthrew the Arians, and received their hate.
They persecuted with satanic zeal,
And made the Saint their rage and anger feel;
But persecution his strong arm nerved
To give the heretics what they deserved;
To vindicate the truth with strength divine,
And make its torch with greater lustre shine.
His potent logic, dialectic skill
Oft made the Saints with exultation thrill,
And every heresy that dared advance
Was made to feel his never-failing lance.
   Of Basil great, and Nazianzen old,
Of John the famous with a mouth of gold,
Whose golden eloquence flowed like the tide,
Whose onward flow swept heresy aside,

And left it like a wreck upon the shore,
To rot, and die, and trouble earth no more,
How shall I speak? Those great and famous men
Need no encomium from so poor a pen.
    What eulogy of man can be expressed
Worthy the glorious Doctors of the West?
Those Latin Fathers as we hear them named,
So learnèd, eloquent, and justly famed?
Ambrose famous in the days of yore,
And *Jerome* deeply skilled in Bible lore,
Surpassing all the Doctors went before,
And all the learnèd Scribes that since have conn'd
The Sacred Scriptures with affection fond?
And *Saint Augustine*, first of all his race,
And first and greatest on the subject, grace,
Who did with learning and with skill profound
The Arians and Pelagians confound;
And on great questions threw a flood of light,
Which leaves to moderns little more to write.
And he, of breadth of mind, and knowledge deep,
The brave defender of Christ's purchased sheep,
The terror of devouring wolves, and bold,
Who would, unchecked, devour the Christian fold,
While yet a Pagan was a sinner base,
And in his person showed the need of grace,
And best could tell its mighty power when
Himself became the holiest of men,
So humble that he should his sins record
For all to read, and glorify the Lord.
And Gregory the Great, whose surname told
His fame and virtues in the days of old,
And told how well he ruled the Christian fold.

Those were the men of learning and of zeal,
To whose great works we Catholics appeal
To know what doctrines early Christians held,
To know in what the early Saints excelled;
And hence it is, that Protestants who doubt,
As do the Ritualists, at length find out
The Church of Rome was then the same as now, }
And so they come to bend the knee and bow, }
And at great sacrifice we must allow. }
But when men see the light, and get a call, }
They should not hesitate, but like St. Paul }
Obey the Lord, although it cost them all }
The world holds dear, a world so soon to end,
And ever proves itself a faithless friend.
    'Twas providential we may clearly see,
That men assailed the Church in infancy,
When zeal and fervour were so burning hot,
And men remembered all the graces got
Through Christ's own teaching, so remembered then,
By zealous, holy, Apostolic men,
Who with th' Apostles had themselves conversed,
And learned their sayings, which they oft rehearsed;
And when Tradition in its youth was clear,
And no deep searching for what then was near.
'Twas Providential too, for men can see
How well the Church's teaching doth agree
With what she taught in her primeval days,
When Gospel truth shone like a brilliant blaze.
We now can see for what the martyrs died,
Though eighteen centuries the times divide;
For they, brave souls, laid down their lives of old
For those same truths which we believe, and hold,

And half of which had long since been destroyed,
If heresy could the covenant make void.
   Let's now consider how the Church expands,
As Constantine extends to her his hands
To raise her up, to dry her briny tears,
Dissolve her fetters, and remove her fears,
And doth moreover aid, and means supply
To raise new Churches, and to beautify;
Not that but she had mighty triumphs gained,
While persecution had her life-blood drained.
In spite of persecution long and dread,
The Church still grew, and wide its branches spread;
In Asia, Africa, and Europe old,
Are millions gathered to the Christian fold.
Tertullian tells us, in a noble strain,
Of its great spread in Britain, Gaul, and Spain;
That thousands there received the Word of God,
In farthest Britain where no Roman trod;
That everywhere throughout the world wide,
Are found disciples of the Crucified.
Irenæus tells "two Germanies" received
The word of God, and piously believed.
And e'en the Goths of Mæsia and of Thrace
Received the faith with all its wondrous grace.
   The Church emerging from her gloomy past,
(Her chains and fetters to the winds are cast,)
Now breathes the air of freedom—gift divine,
And mounts the throne with noble Constantine,
(Not that but thrones are dangerous in their way,
And they who mount them have more need to pray.)
And then begins her grand and social reign,
To raise the fallen, break the captives' chain.

And like the sun, to flood the earth with light,
A light which shows us what is just and right,
And what is wicked, sinful, and profane,
And every vice from which we should refrain,
To make us happy e'en on earth below,
Amidst its trials, misery, and woe.

    To her Our Lord a grand commission gave
To teach mankind, to preach, baptize, and save,
To heal the wounded, and their sins forgive,
Dispensing graces that her sons may live
A life of sanctity; and to bestow
On suffering man a balm for every woe;
To offer sacrifice for daily faults,
And strengthen souls 'gainst Satan's dread assaults,
Protecting innocence, and healing vice,
Whate'er the cost, the labour, or the price;
Erecting hospitals to lighten woes,
To soothe the sorrows of both friends and foes,
For heavenly charity no distinction knows.
Each Christian's heart becomes a mercy-seat,
And wealthy nobles wash the pilgrims' feet,
For they, since freed from Pride's unholy leaven,
Regard the humble as the heirs of Heaven,
And objects dearest to His heart divine,
Who makes His sun on all alike to shine,
And with "the poor in spirit" shares His throne,
For they become His heirs, and they alone;
And hence the Church for ever loves the poor,
And does her best their many ills to cure;
She asks the poor their poverty to bear,
And asks the rich with them their wealth to share;
And like St. Paul, she gathers alms to send
To those in need, to succour and befriend.

She ever comforts and consoles the sick,
And visits them with ready step and quick;
Makes no distinction between rich and poor,
Though pomp and wealth may senseless souls allure.
Both high and low at all her altars meet,
And humbly kneel to kiss the Saviour's feet
When He comes down, and on the altar rests,
And comes to dwell within their loving breasts.

See what the Church since early youth has done,
Although her life has been a chequered one;
She built up schools and colleges to shed
The light of science, and its rays to spread
O'er nations, kingdoms, islands far and near,
Where darkness reigned, and superstitious fear,
And where the name Jehovah was unknown,
And men fell down to worship stick and stone.
She taught proud kings to justly rule and reign,
And from injustice subjects to restrain.
She taught all subjects wisely to obey,
And to their rulers lawful tribute pay.

And who has raised those temples we behold
So grand, majestic, venerable, old?
Not surely heretics, who passed away,
Nor yet reformers of a later day.
To build new churches never was their plan,
But plunder old ones, when and where they can.

The Church now raised to influence and power,
Enjoying fully freedom's kingly dower,
Scatters blessings never known before,
Diffusing happiness from shore to shore.
Old heathen laws, so cruel and unjust,
Are Christianised, old manners cleansed from rust

Are now become both polished and refined,
Since Christian teaching elevates the mind
Above the pleasures of the passing hour,
And human feelings feel the Church's power.
The *Law of Nations*, once the law of might,
Is now become the Christian law of right,
A law of clemency, a law of love,
A law of mercy coming from above.

   Wars are no more for slaves and booty made,
For justice only are their hosts arrayed.
Prisoners of war are made no longer slaves,
Or sacrificed upon their Conqueror's graves.

   What Church but Rome's proclaimed the Gospel law,
While still no enemy can find a flaw
In her definitions when she expounds
The Word of God, and heresy confounds?
Has she recalled a single word she said
To humble heresy, and crush its head?
What Church but Rome's preserved with loving care,
The Holy Bible as a treasure rare?
For ages long, while printing was unknown,
'Twas she preserved the Word of God, and she alone.
Many a year in some *Scriptorium* old,
Her zealous monks had toiled in heat and cold,
And traced with patient love from age to age,
And copied skilfully the sacred page,
And writings of the Fathers one and all,
And e'en the authors which we classic call.
And these were nought but "lazy Monks," forsooth,
With our "Reformers"—not too famed for truth,
Who plundered first, and then repaid with lies
The holy monks, so hateful in their eyes.

Well might they call them "*lazy and supine*,"
To plunder whom appeared a work divine
In th' opinion of " Reformers" great,
Whose love of plunder e'en surpassed their hate
Of Rome's religion, and the Pope its Head;
Whom all the heretics both fear and dread.

The Church, developed now and organized,
Her wondrous plans for human needs devised,
Began that structure which we view with awe,
And which men call her Code of Canon Law.
'Tis hard to tell in easy flowing rhyme
The great perfections of this Code sublime
Concerning holy places, persons, things,
And teaching Rulers, Bishops, Popes, and Kings
To rule and legislate as best they can
For God's great glory, and the good of man;
And teaching subjects to obey, and give
To God due glory if they wish to live
With Him hereafter 'bove the starry sphere—
A great reward for having served Him here.

We've seen the Church's sufferings and her tears,
And triumphs too, the first three hundred years,
And now let's view the ones that next succeed,
As she became from penal fetters freed;
And see how well the Gospel light she spread,
How well she fought with potent foes, and dread;
With royal Arians, and Apostates too,
Who did their best her mission to undo.
By royal favour Arians grow strong,
Renew their onslaught, and the war prolong;
And have recourse to cunning arts and wiles,
To win by flattery and deceitful smiles

The great and powerful to help their cause
By royal favour, and by penal laws.
They gained the son of Constantine the Great,
And many Bishops, shameful to relate.
Constantius (Arian), son of Constantine,
A despot great delays not to combine
With Arian Bishops; and at Rimini
Was guilty of the greatest tyranny
O'er holy Bishops who in council met,
And were encompassed by the royal net,
And robbed of freedom, and compelled to do
What they lamented, and were known to rue.
(They thought perhaps their course was orthodox,
Beguiled by Arians cunning as the fox),
When from the tyrant they obtained release,
They all again professed the faith of Nice.
The Arian Bishops, numbering fourscore,
Remained the same as they had been before.
The Orthodox Bishops were as four to one,
When sat the Council and its work begun;
But seven long months of close captivity
Made most of them with Arian eyes to see,
And made them sign what they refused when free.
They soon were censured, and their work reversed
By Pope Liberius and the Church dispersed.
But though the tyrant did his very best,
And introduced a new religious test
To strengthen heresy, and to uproot
The Faith of Christ, he but increased its fruit!
The Church still triumphs, and extends her hands,
To scatter blessings over heathen lands;
To preach salvation as with trumpet loud,
To raise the fallen, and restrain the proud,

To heal, to nurse, to care poor fallen man,
And be to all the good Samaritan.

Arius gave her opposition great,
But he, though cunning, shared the common fate
Of all heresiarchs who bray and brawl,
Until Rome's thunderbolts upon them fall,
And they begin to wither, and to rot,
Their sins detested, and themselves forgot.

Arius, whose heresy whole kingdoms overran,
Was a learnèd, able, and ambitious man,
And fond of novelty, and proud, and vain,
And anxious, too, high honours to obtain;
And with that hope to Alexandria came,
Where he acquired an unenvied fame;
And by deceiving got himself ordained,
And thus the Sacraments, I fear, profaned!
He taught the Son of God (rank blasphemy)
Did not exist from all eternity,
And was like one of Adam's sinful race,
But that He did a holy life embrace,
And God rewarded Him, and made Him share
In His own nature, so divinely fair;
And by His merits, He the titles won
Of "The Word," "The Wisdom of the Father," and
    "The Son."

A blacker heresy yet never spread,
And hard it was to crush its serpent-head;
A head of craft, of cunning, and intrigue,
So much with hell and wickedness in league,
So Proteus-like, so tortuous in its ways,
And so remarkable for length of days.
Its author's awful, dreadful, sudden death
Did not deprive it or of life or breath.

This subtle heresy, condemned so oft,
And which blasphemed our Lord—at whom it scoffed—
Under Constantius made progress east and west,
By sycophantic Bishops long caressed.
It persecuted when and where it could
The Bishops who its violence withstood;
And first and greatest of its mortal foes
Was Athanasius, as the world knows,
The greatest champion of God's truth divine,
Who did such knowledge, learning, skill, combine
In war with error which his skill confessed,
While truth acknowledges his sword the best.
He was exiled—driven from his See—
And many other Bishops well as he.
Constantius, the son of Constantine,
Delays not with the Arians to join
Against the Orthodox; by his decrees
Ninety Bishops driven from their Sees
In Egypt, are by Arians replaced,
And Athanasius, like a felon chased,
Made his escape, and to the desert fled,
A price still set upon his holy head!
  Though long the fight, the Arians had to yield,
And leave the Church quite mistress of the field.
Though long they struggled, and though hard they fought,
God's curse o'ertook them, and they came to nought,
Except that Luther later disinterred
So many errors of all sects that erred.
  Ere the fourth century had reached its close,
Another class of enemies arose
T' assail the Church, and if they could, destroy,
Who did strong weapons for that end employ—

Wealth and power, and legislation fell,
The arms of flesh—the armoury of hell;
And eloquence, also sharper than the spear,
And which could ridicule, and scoff, and jeer
At everything that Catholics revere.

Apostate princes sprung from Christian kings,
With all the malice that from hatred springs,
In every age since then the Church assail,
And like the heretics are doomed to fail.
The Church shall stand and see the end of all,
Since all her enemies are doomed to fall.

The first, most wicked, of the class I named,
Was Julian Emperor, Apostate famed ;
First Christian Emperor, who had the will
To strike the Church, his Mother, and to kill ;
And then those filthy idols to restore,
Which cursed the earth for centuries before !
This wicked scourge, so poisoned in his youth
By wicked teaching, and dislike of truth,
Loved Pagan idols, and the magic art—
Strong indications of a perverse heart—
Abjured religion, and the Church deprived
Of all her privileges, and revived
Old Pagan worship, and the gods restored,
Which Pagan Rome so slavishly adored.
He robbed the Church, her pensions all suppressed,
By which she helped the feeble and distressed,
Forbade all Christians at the Bar to plead,
Or hold positions that might serve their creed ;
To teach the sciences, or books to write,
T' impart instruction, or to spread the light ;

F

So that dark ignorance might spread its pall
O'er all the Christians, and their souls enthral—
Too good he thought for "Galileans" all!
(To make just one reflection here I pause,
A model *his* for barbarous Penal laws,
A model which our legislators took,
When our "Reformers" Peter's Barque forsook,)
But thinking these were methods rather slow,
And wishing to inflict a mortal blow
By showing that the ancient Prophets lied,
That Christ's own words would not be verified,
Resolved to build the Temple, and restore
(And not through love) its worship as of yore.
To prove that Christ had not the future known,
When He foretold a stone upon a stone
Would not be left of all that Temple grand,
So old, so honoured, and divinely planned,
He gave the Jews encouragement and aid,
Who at His bidding foolishly essayed
Their ancient glorious Temple to rebuild ;
And they, not thinking, literally fulfilled
The Word of Christ, for when the ground was cleared,
And Jews rejoicing no disaster feared,
And they to lay the stones with joy began,
A sudden flame among the workmen ran,
And like an earthquake's burning breath it spread,
Prevented work, and filled the men with dread,
Who soon deserted, and in terror fled ;
And as historians—Pagans too—record,
Fulfilled the prophecy of Christ Our Lord !
And yet this miracle did not abate
The zeal of Julian, or relax his hate

Against the Christians, whom his rage appalled,
And in derision *Galileans* called !
He his fury for awhile restrained,
Till he a victory o'er the Persians gained.
In sight of victory saying, "All is ours,"
While darts were falling in terrific showers,
Death seized the victor through a fatal dart,
And while his life-blood issued from his heart,
He took a handful, and at Heaven cast.
" Thou hast conquered, *Galilean,*" were the last
Words uttered by this pest of hell—
May all Apostates on their meaning dwell.
    Whilst Christ's own Church is saddened by her kings,
Her greatest glory from the desert springs ;
Her greatest bulwark 'gainst the rage of hell
Are her poor hermits, who in deserts dwell,
And her chaste cenobites, whose prayers fly
To her protection, and which pierce the sky,
And won't depart till God Most High behold,
And send all succour to the Christian fold.
The monks who fly the world and all its strife,
And lead a mortified and humble life,
And who with charity and fervour glow,
Chaste as angels, spotless as the snow,
Dead to the world, and all its pomp and pride,
And with the thought of Heaven occupied ;
Who give their days to fasting and to prayer,
Who live upon the poorest, coarsest fare,
Their garments hair-cloth, and their bed the ground—
Their souls aflame with piety profound—
These are the Church's heroes, these her boast,
These are the riches that she values most,

Beyond the smiles of all the kings that reign;
These are the wheat of God, the golden grain
Which Christ shall gather to the courts above,
The home of glory and of endless love.
  Blessed they among Christ's ransomed sheep
Who all the counsels of perfection keep,
Who sell their goods, and give them to the poor,
And follow Christ, salvation to secure,
Who fast, and pray, and lonely vigils keep,
And for their sins, and those of others weep;
Such was St. Paul the hermit, child of grace,
And Anthony, father of a saintly race
Of holy monks who live for God alone,
And make the light of sanctity be known,
And show how easy Heaven may be won
By Christian Athletes, who in earnest run,
Who strip themselves of all things, and despise
The goods of earth, to gain the wished-for prize.
And who was Paul of whom so much is said,
And who for safety to the desert fled,
When Decius persecuted young and old
For having joined the early Christian Fold?
Paul was born in two hundred twenty-nine,
And in his youth received a call divine
To quit the world, and to the desert fly
To save his soul, and reach his home on high.
He sought the desert, and he found a cave
Wherein to dwell, and grace and mercy crave.
A palm-tree sheltered him, and gave him food,
And of its leaves he made his garments rude.
This second Moses living in his cave
Had nought to eat but what the palm-tree gave,

Until he reached the age of forty-three,
A wondrous life of holy poverty !
And was thenceforth miraculously fed
By a raven bringing him his daily bread !
And here he lived for ninety passing years,
Dead to the world, and all its hopes and fears,
Serving God and serving Him alone,
As do the angels who surround His Throne,
And praying for the Church he loved so well,
That she might triumph o'er the hosts of hell.
Now growing old, and coming near his end,
With no one near to succour or befriend,
God sent to him another holy soul
To comfort, care, attend him and console.
That soul was Anthony, who also fled
A wicked world, and all its dangers dread.
Paul took not long to settle his accounts,
And soon he dies and up to glory mounts;
He reached the age of five score years and ten,
And dies the poorest of the sons of men.
Of his approaching end he calmly spoke,
And asked to have St. Athanasius' cloak ;
And Anthony travelled back the cloak to bring,
And on his way he heard the angels sing
As they accompanied the soul of Paul
To glory's height to meet the God of all.
He wraps his body in the cloak, and laid
It in the grave two friendly lions made :
And having left him in his house of clay,
His palm leaf tunic gladly bore away.
And, wonder not, dear reader, God is kind
To all who serve Him with an earnest mind.

And who was Anthony, this light of lights,
This saintly father of all cenobites?
This wondrous monk, of Holy Church the son,
Was in Egypt born—two hundred fifty-one;
Was rich, was noble, sold his goods, and gave
To help the needy, and with courage brave
Fled to the desert, where he chose a grave
To be his residence for twenty years,
Which he bedewed with penitential tears;
And twice a year in this far-off retreat
A friend to nourish brought him food to eat.
Anthony then fled farther from the sight
Of mortal man, and on the mountain's height
He found a ruined castle—cheerless dome—
And well nigh twenty years made it his home;
But during Dioclesian's wicked reign
Many seek him, and with him remain
To give themselves to God, as he had done,
And fly the world, and all its dangers shun;
And monasteries arose around the mount,
So great the number one could scarcely count,
Since full ten thousand sought this holy school,
When St. Serapion began to rule.
Those monks and hermits lead secluded lives
In cells adjoining, as do bees in hives,
Observing silence, save in holy prayer,
And speaking only on occasions rare.
For death St. Anthony was well prepared,
And all his goods—his cloak and sheepskins—shared
With St. Athanasius and Serapion,
While round his death-bed every virtue shone,
And God's own angels smiled his couch upon.

Did ever heresy, and view them all,
Produce such saints as Anthony and Paul,
Who offered violence to sin and vice,
Who purchased Heaven, and who paid the price?
They bore the Cross, the body mortified,
They followed Jesus, and themselves denied;
Their monkish virtues but excite the bile
Of Churches false who hate them and revile.
The Church wherein such heavenly virtues grew
Must surely be the Holy and the True.

The humble Muse now plods her way along,
And weaves a garland of religious song;
But all unworthy of the Mystic Bride
Of Him whose robes with Precious Blood were dyed.
But let the reader clearly understand
These are but shells she gathers on the strand.
What earthly Muse with all her gifts divine
Can tell the history of Peter's line?
Can paint its trials, and its triumphs tell
O'er persecutions from the gates of hell?
I give but glimpses as I pass along,
And plait a wreath of very simple song,
But quite unworthy to adorn the brows
Of our dear Mother—Christ's Eternal Spouse.

END OF PART II.

Printed by EDMUND BURKE & Co., 61 & 62 Great Strand St., Dublin.

WORKS BY THE SAME AUTHOR.

◆

Temperance Songs and Lyrics.
Third Edition.
Crown 8vo, Printed Cover, 1s.; Cloth, 1s. 6d.

Intemperance; or the Evils of Drink.
A Poem.
Fourth Edition. Crown 8vo, Printed Cover, 6d.; Cloth, 9d.

Our Thirst for Drink; Its Cause and Cure.
Second Edition.
Crown 8vo, Printed Cover, 1s.; Cloth, 1s. 6d.

NOTE.—"Temperance Songs and Lyrics," "Intemperance," and "Our Thirst for Drink" may be had in one volume, cloth, 2s. 6d.

Paddy Blake among the Soupers.
Third Edition.
Crown 8vo, Printed Cover, 4d.; Cloth, 1s.

Verses on Devotional and Doctrinal Subjects.
Three Vols. bound in one, cloth, red edges,
net, 3s. 6d.

Three Vols. bound in one, cloth, gilt edges, *net*, 4s.

JAMES DUFFY & CO., LTD., 15 WELLINGTON QUAY, DUBLIN.

www.ingramcontent.com/pod-product-compliance
Lightning Source LLC
Chambersburg PA
CBHW020255090426
42735CB00009B/1097